THE ULTIMATE GUIDE TO
RAISING A PUPPY

How to Train and Care for Your New Dog

Victoria Stilwell

TEN SPEED PRESS
California | New York

Copyright © 2019 by Victoria Stilwell, Inc.

Published in the United States by Ten Speed Press, an imprint of
Random House, a division of Penguin Random House LLC, New York.
www.crownpublishing.com
www.tenspeed.com

Ten Speed Press and the Ten Speed Press colophon are registered
trademarks of Penguin Random House LLC.

Front cover photograph copyright © Getty Images / Bigandt_Photography

Library of Congress Cataloging-in-Publication Data
Names: Stilwell, Victoria, author.
Title: The ultimate guide to raising a puppy : how to train and care
    for your new dog / Victoria Stilwell.
Description: First edition. | New York : Ten Speed Press, [2019] |
    Includes bibliographical references and index.
Identifiers: LCCN 2019019898| ISBN 9780399582455 (trade paperback) |
    ISBN 9780399582462 (ebook)
Subjects: LCSH: Puppies. | Puppies—Training.
Classification: LCC SF427 .S86 2019 | DDC 636.7/07—dc23
    LC record available at https://lccn.loc.gov/2019019898

Trade Paperback ISBN: 978-0-399-58245-5
eBook ISBN: 978-0-399-58246-2

Printed in the United States of America

Design by Nemo Liu

10 9 8 7 6 5 4 3 2 1

First Edition

THE ULTIMATE GUIDE TO RAISING A PUPPY

🐾🐾🐾 FOR OUR BELOVED SADIE 🐾🐾🐾

CONTENTS

Preface   ix

Introduction   1

CHAPTER 1   **Before the Beginning**   8

Early Development • Enrichment and Brain
Development • Picking Your Puppy

CHAPTER 2   **Everything's a First**   25

Preparation and Safety • Bringing Puppy Home • The
Right Equipment • What Your Puppy Wants • Building a
Bond • Giving Your Puppy Choices • The Loud Puppy •
The Healthy Puppy • Feeding Your Puppy

CHAPTER 3   **Teaching Life Skills**   65

Raising a Resilient Puppy • Handling Your Puppy •
Coping with Human Greeting Behavior • Training Your
Puppy • Communicating with Your Puppy • Puppy
Language • Decoding Vocal Language • Chewing Skills •
Nipping and Mouthing Skills • Toileting Skills • Recall
Skills (Coming When Called) • Play Skills • Social Skills •
Walking Skills • Leash Skills

CHAPTER 4 Empowering Your Puppy   122
🐾 🐾 🐾 🐾
The Power of Choice • Intelligence and the Five Cognitive
Dimensions • The Power of Sense • Preventing Fear
Behavior • Choice-Centered Training • What Would Your
Puppy Say?

CHAPTER 5 The Ups and Downs of Adolescence   163
🐾 🐾 🐾 🐾 🐾
Adolescent Exuberance • Adolescent Fear • Impulsivity •
Reactivity • Neutering • Scent Marking • Humping •
Mine! • Muzzle Training • Providing Enrichment

Afterword: Living in Harmony with Your Dog   192
Acknowledgments   201
Resources   202
Endnotes   203
About the Author   209
Index   210

PREFACE

My beautiful, big brown dog lifts up her wise old head and looks at me with kind, loving eyes. These two intensely dark pools have seen sixteen years of life, a long time for a dog, and as I gaze into them I recall all the wonderful memories we have had together. Summer days exploring the North Georgia mountains, family birthday celebrations, and winter nights spent in front of the fire. Those eyes have seen our family grow through the years, witnessing the good times and commiserating with the hard ones. Sadie has been with us every step of the way. She is the rock we can always depend on to lighten our load, to greet us warmly when we come home from work, and to give us love.

Sadie came into our lives when she was five years old, a gentle girl who seemed wise beyond her years. She is a calm dog in the house and a wild huntress outside. She sees the world through her magnificent nose and is driven by secret odors that lead her on intense investigations I wish I could understand. Sadie knows the neighborhood news before I do. She knows what dogs have passed by, what animals have been in the area, and who has been jogging that morning. If I could speak her language, I know we would gossip for hours.

I didn't know Sadie when she was a puppy, but I can only imagine how beautiful she was. Sadie lived with an elderly lady who had recently lost her husband. The family hoped to ease their mother's loneliness by getting her a companion, and even though an energetic, excitable Labrador puppy was not necessarily the best idea for an elderly person, what Sadie lacked in exercise and social experiences with other dogs, she got back a hundred-fold in love. Scarlet raised Sadie for five years until Scarlet sadly passed away. A week later a trainer friend of mine, Joyce Hagan, brought the gorgeous chocolate Labrador to our house to see if we wanted to adopt her. Sadie never left.

I have no doubt that Scarlet's love and kindness in those important puppy and adolescent years makes Sadie so good with people, just as I am certain that Sadie's lack of canine social experiences makes her uncomfortable around other dogs. I see a lot of her past by watching her behavior in the present, but I wish I could have been there at the beginning when my beautiful girl came into the world. I can only imagine what she was like as a puppy. Cheeky, inquisitive, energetic, loving, impulsive—she must have brought such joy to everyone. I wish I had known her then and stolen five more years with the best dog in the world.

Sadie is one of the reasons I'm writing this book. I want to explore what she must have been like as a puppy and in doing so take you on a journey into your puppy's world. So I'm going back in time, to where Sadie started out on her amazing journey, sixteen years ago.

INTRODUCTION

Puppies! We all love them, but along with those cute faces and wiggly tails comes a whole host of challenges that make raising a puppy as overwhelming as it is joyful. With so much available but conflicting information out there, it can be very hard for pet parents to know what advice to follow. Where should I get my puppy from? How will I get him to sleep through the night? How long does it take to toilet train my puppy? What is the difference between puppy nipping and biting? How can I successfully introduce a new pup to my kids?

I answer these questions and many more throughout this book, but I also focus on something that is just as important. I call it the how and the why. Understanding how your puppy experiences the world and why she behaves in a certain way will help you raise her correctly. So while this book is a practical support system and a go-to source of information when you are up in the middle of the night wondering how to get your whining puppy to go to sleep or when you are on your knees cleaning up the latest accident, it also helps you understand just how incredible your puppy is. Yes, raising a puppy is challenging, but these challenges are worth it when you hold that bundle of energy in your arms and feel such love that your heart might explode. *The Ultimate Guide to Raising a Puppy* is with you every step of the way.

My Story

I have a passion for dogs and have always been fascinated by their behavior. As a member of an enormous international dog-loving club, I live with and celebrate these incredible animals every day. I am constantly amazed by the fact that dogs are the most successful domestic species on the planet and have successfully evolved with humans over thousands of years. This is an incredible achievement on both sides. Humans have adapted to having dogs in their lives, and we have honed the skills of these effective predators in many different ways. But while we congratulate ourselves for making such a beneficial alliance, we also need to respect the journey made by the dog, which is nothing short of remarkable. Dogs have gone from hunting and fending for themselves to sharing our beds and eating our food. They don't speak our language or understand most of our rules, but they still manage to adapt to our complicated lives. Humans are not easy to live with, but dogs, for the most part, successfully negotiate the challenges we give them.

I have been a dog trainer and behavior consultant for twenty years, starting out in some of what I still believe are the toughest environments for dogs to live in—the cities of London and New York. Relocating to the United States from the UK was a big leap for me in many respects, but the challenges I faced training puppies and adult dogs in a city that only allows dogs off leash in cramped dog runs or in Central Park before 9 a.m. meant that I worked with dogs that not only were incredibly frustrated and reactive, but had developed a whole host of anxieties exacerbated by city living: noise phobias, space issues, separation distress, aggressive behavior toward people and other dogs, touch sensitivities, destructive chewing, and incessant barking, to name but a few.

But for all its faults, Manhattan can also be the best place to have a dog. The city might be an overwhelming assault on all the senses, but it's a delicious smorgasbord of ever-changing smells that provide countless hours of wonder for nose-driven dogs. Teaching dogs to focus on streets crowded with people, sirens and horns blaring every few minutes, and a myriad of distracting smells from garbage, human waste, and city rats, taught me to be very patient and provided ample opportunity to work with many different and complex canine behavior issues in an unforgiving environment.

I loved the challenge of working with my canine and human clients in the city, but because of the difficult environment we all lived in, I focused a lot of my time on teaching methods that would prevent behavior problems from occurring in the first place. Techniques designed to instill coping skills and therefore confidence in adults could also be used to great effectiveness with puppies. New Yorkers don't worry about the size of their living spaces, and Great Danes live as comfortably in one-bedroom apartments as pugs and Yorkshire terriers. These dogs benefit from a lot more attention, it seems, than dogs in the suburbs, because at a minimum, their human caregivers have to take them outside to toilet three to four times a day. It was easy for my puppy clients to become housetrained quickly with well-crafted schedules and diligent care. These puppies didn't seem to mind the hustle and bustle of a busy city and enjoyed the constant attention received from inquisitive dogs and passersby. The city itself seemed to offer the perfect stress inoculation, with daily exposure that naturally taught the pups to cope well in social situations. Raising a puppy in New York City was not as difficult as I had first feared.

In late 2004, I created a TV show called *It's Me or the Dog* that became very popular around the world and took over my life for eight seasons, filmed over ten years. Because of the success of the show and the subsequent platform it provided, I was able to get the message out about a more humane way of teaching puppies and dogs of all breeds, drives, and with all kinds of behavior problems.

Then a chance meeting with an experienced K9 handler from the Gwinnett County Sheriff's K9 unit in Georgia led me into the world of police K9. I had already worked with accelerant detection canines, or arson dogs, for the State Farm Arson Dog program but wanted to understand more about the lives of police dogs and their handlers. Having spent a few months attending training seminars and reading all I could about the subject, I started developing a successful web series called *Guardians of the Night*. The show was initially conceived to explore the state of police dog training in the United States, but it turned into much more. To understand the experience of handlers and their dogs, I had to experience it for myself, and the five years of being immersed in the daily lives of these brave officers and their dogs gave me a new perspective and appreciation for the work they do.

I still work with police and other working dogs, following their growth from lanky adolescents to courageous adults, and my experience in the working and companion dog world has proven to me that there is no difference in the way a working dog or a pet dog can and should be taught. They both have the same desires, they learn in the same way and have the same need to feel safe and secure. Whatever role your puppy fulfills in your life, never forget that you are a team and the learning is the same. Different jobs obviously require different skills, but most dogs have bionic noses whether we hone their sniffy skills to detect the odor of narcotics or to play scent games at home. Puppy raising follows similar guidelines for all dogs in whatever roles they eventually serve.

I love working with puppies. These little bundles of energy are blank slates that are eager to lap up and experience anything they can. Their vitality and energy for life fills me with hope and happiness, and I consider it a privilege to help guide pups and their people through the first part of life because early guidance determines a puppy's ultimate success.

ANIMAL ATTRACTION

I have just returned from the daily walk with my adult dogs, which inevitably ends up being a social event judging by the number of people I talk to while walking. I usually walk in the local park, which takes me past a playground. My dogs are used to having children run up and want to touch them, and I have taught them to cope with this scenario. Even if I decide to go on a different route, I always bump into people who want to interact with my dogs. Sadie and Jasmine not only bring joy to me, they also bring joy to complete strangers.

Part of our attraction to dogs, and puppies in particular, is innate. Researchers from Rutgers University in New Jersey revealed that when given the choice, toddlers between one and three years old will spend more time interacting with live animals than with inanimate toys.[1] Research has also found that neurons in the amygdala, the brain's emotional center, respond preferentially to animal images.[2] Humans have positive responses to beings with characteristics typical of human infants—such as wide, large eyes and big foreheads. Baby animals produce the same instinctive responses in us as human babies do.

Our attraction to dogs is also cultural. While many of us in the West celebrate these amazing animals and live with them in our homes, other cultures see dogs as unclean and carriers of disease. We are influenced by the cultures we live in, and if our friends and neighbors have a dog or get a new puppy, we are more likely to get one ourselves. We're also attracted to the latest media sensations. After the film *101 Dalmatians* hit movie theaters, everyone wanted a dalmatian, but the shelters quickly filled up with discarded puppies and adolescent dogs when people realized what an energetic breed they were. It's very sad that when a movie focuses on a certain breed, the shelters have to open their doors to the latest discarded canine trend.

Dogs are also very useful, and that is partly why they have evolved so successfully with us for thousands of years. They were and still are good hunting and guarding partners, helping us find food and protecting our homes, crops, and livestock. We have harnessed their skills to help us detect human and animal diseases, and now dogs are being used in even more extraordinary ways by helping us conserve our planet—the subject of my latest TV show, *Dogs with Extraordinary Jobs*.

But let's look at this attachment more closely. A dog's attachment to a human is like a child's to a parent. In fact, puppies and adult dogs behave in a similar way to young children if they are left alone with someone they don't know. A "strange situation test" has tested attachment theory in children. If a child is in a strange environment with a known adult and some toys to play with, the child is more likely to walk away from the adult and confidently play. If the known adult walks out of view and the child is left with an adult they don't know, they stop play and anxiously await the known adult's return. When puppies, adolescents, and adult dogs were put through a similar test, it was no surprise that they behaved in exactly the same way.[3]

Dogs and people also share similar behavioral responses to emotion. Dogs seem to display jealous behavior when they guard a resource or monopolize a person's attention. The definition of human jealousy includes phrases such as "vigilance in maintaining or guarding something," and "resentment against a rival." This certainly explains why we alarm our cars and houses and are pushy, resentful, and competitive when we think someone poses a threat to things we have or people that are important to us. It's very common for dogs to push themselves between hugging couples or invade the space of another dog that is being petted. In fact, the presence of human caregivers can sometimes cause fights between dogs that are competing for human attention.

At the end of the day, our dogs are our beloved companions. The emotional connection we feel toward them might be even stronger than the one we feel for human family members. Dogs don't judge us, answer back, or lie—in fact, they are the source of comfort that many people crave.

As well as being good for our social life, dogs make us healthier. Not only do we exercise more if we have a dog, a study of ninety-two people at the University of Pennsylvania showed that people who had pets were more likely to be alive a year after a heart attack than those who did not have a companion animal.[4] Dogs are great stress relievers and have an incredible ability to make us feel better.

CHAPTER 1

Before the Beginning

Before we get to the beginning of your puppy's journey with you, there's a "before the beginning." And it is this "before" that provides the very foundation for your puppy's personality. Most people who adopt or buy a puppy don't have the luxury of knowing who the parents are, but where a puppy is born and how she is raised plays a significant role in creating her particular personality, and that is why it's important to understand her process right from the start, regardless of how she came into your life.

Early Development

Genes provide the blueprint for a dog's appearance, temperament, and behavior. If you have a purebred Labrador, for example, he most certainly comes from Lab parents. But just because he looks like a Labrador doesn't mean that he will necessarily behave like one; the environment he is raised in has a very powerful influence on how genes are expressed. You might open a breed book about German shepherds and see that they are predisposed to guard, are highly sound sensitive, and have a tendency to be nervous, but not all German shepherds guard, just as not every Labrador is good with children, despite what the breed-centric books might tell you. Because dogs of the same breed are born to different parents in diverse climates and situations, behavior that is influenced by their genetic makeup can change depending on their environmental and situational experiences. Therefore, the temperament and behavior of dogs of the same breed can be very different.

All my dogs are from rescue situations, so I've never known their parents or how they were conceived. I am pretty sure that Sadie's parents were both chocolate Labradors because Sadie looks like a chocolate Labrador. Jasmine, my Chihuahua, is definitely a mix of something, but one of her parents had to be a Chihuahua. (We think her other parent was a meerkat because she looks so much like one, except that makes for a confusing picture at conception—so maybe min pin [miniature pinscher] or some kind of small terrier/rat-looking thing. . . . Sorry, Jasmine!)

Puppy genes are certainly influenced by the genes of their parents, but the experiences of the pregnant mother can have a profound effect on the puppies she carries in her womb. Mothers that are healthy and live in calm, enriching environments have a greater chance of producing mentally and physically healthy puppies than mothers who are sick or live in stressful environments. If a mother is stressed while she is pregnant, her puppies might grow up to be nervy and fearful. Research has shown that if a mother is stressed during the final third of her pregnancy, her pups can be severely emotionally reactive. The mother's production of stress hormones during this sensitive period will truly influence her puppies.[1]

A puppy can also be affected by littermates in the womb. I certainly see many male-typical behaviors in Jasmine. She marks outside, lifts her leg to urinate, and humps Sadie's hind leg—although the humping only occurs when Sadie is lying down chewing on a bone or toy that Jasmine wants. It seems that Jasmine is using the action of humping as a way of getting Sadie's attention or of distracting her from chewing on her bone so Jasmine can steal it. These male-typical behaviors could be because Jasmine's brain was influenced by the puppies that were developing next to her in the womb. Research shows that if there are more male than female puppies in the womb, male hormones called androgens can leak out into the embryonic fluid, affecting the other pups. Females that are born in male-dominant litters tend to show more masculine-type behaviors than female pups born in female-dominant litters. This suggests that hormones do have a profound effect on the developing brains of puppies in the womb.[2]

Developmental periods are crucial stages of a dog's behavioral and cognitive development and learning. A puppy's behavioral and cognitive future can be shaped through positive and negative exposure to novel stimuli engaging all their senses within the environment.

NEONATAL (BIRTH TO TWO WEEKS)

At birth, the ears and eyes of your puppy are closed. However, his touch sense is active and his sense of smell quickly develops and draws him to feed from his mother. Even though your puppy's brain is very small and immature at this age, simple learning is still possible and daily handling can accelerate your puppy's maturation, motor coordination, and problem-solving skills. In fact, puppies that have been handled and mildly stressed by human handling tend to be better at coping with novelty and are more emotionally stable as they grow into adults.[3]

As soon as a puppy is born, he relies on touch to find his mother, to stimulate milk flow for feeding, and as a source of comfort. Mothers lick and nuzzle their puppies from birth, improving the puppies' circulation and encouraging them to eliminate waste in order to stay healthy. Licking and touch helps form emotional bonds between mom and her pups, and if a puppy experiences human touch from birth, this helps that puppy to develop social attachments with people as he grows. At this stage, puppies spend most of the time sleeping close to one another, gaining warmth and safety from their littermates and sustenance from their mother.

TRANSITIONAL PERIOD (TWO TO THREE WEEKS)

This period of development is one of rapid growth and change. Eyes begin to open at the beginning of this stage, which may start at anywhere from ten to sixteen days of age. Ear canals open at the end of this period, usually a week after the eyes open, at about twenty days. Teeth also emerge at around nineteen to twenty days of age, and your puppy's behavior begins to change during this period as she transitions between the neonatal and socialization phases. Behaviors that are seen during the transitional stage may include crawling backward and forward, standing, walking, and voiding without being licked by her mother. Pups also start play fighting with littermates.

PRIMARY SOCIALIZATION (THREE TO FIVE WEEKS)

At this stage your puppy is learning how to communicate with other dogs, and bite inhibition is learned through play. Bite inhibition teaches pups about bite pressure and what pressure might elicit a negative response from littermates. This feedback is important as it starts your puppy on the journey to a softer mouth or at least enables your puppy to gain an understanding of what pressure might be too hard. Puppies are also more inclined to interact with humans during this period, especially if there has been appropriate handling from birth. Removing a puppy from the litter completely during this primary socialization period can result in behavior disorders, such as separation anxiety, compulsive disorders, fear, and aggression.

A shift happens at about four to five weeks old that starts the weaning process. It's at this time that the mother sometimes walks away from her pups as they nurse. This disconnection starts the puppies' transition from complete dependency on mom to independent social beings that have to negotiate a social order.

Disconnection can have a profound effect on the puppy's emotional well-being, but the more resilient the puppy is, the easier it is to make the adjustment. Studies have shown that the more punishing and threatening the mother is to her pups during the disconnection process, the less socially confident her puppies will be toward strange people. Mothers that are gentler toward their pups and use less threatening behavior during the weaning process tend to have pups that are more socially confident toward people and other animals and can cope better in strange environments. If a mother does not give important feedback on bite strength or other social behaviors at this stage, pups can be difficult to teach as they grow, so gentle guidance from mom is important.[4]

SECONDARY SOCIALIZATION (SIX TO TWELVE WEEKS)

Puppies continue to learn social skills as they adapt to the human world, and positive, proactive socialization should now begin in safe, controlled situations. Puppies can learn to interact with and receive rewards such as praise, play, toys, and puppy-appropriate food from humans. Human and puppy play during this period continues to teach appropriate play and interactions.

Your puppy's first social partners are likely to be her siblings, and she will learn vital social skills through social interaction and play. Feedback from her mother and siblings provides a foundation for you to build on, and, for a few important weeks, your puppy will learn from the responses she receives to things that she does. If she bites another puppy too hard during play, she will receive information from the other puppy or the mother that her bite is too hard and she will begin to inhibit her bite. If puppies are removed too early from mom and littermates, they won't get this valuable feedback and could have "hard mouths" as a result.

Social learning around food also begins at this time. While puppies are still feeding from their mother, they are very close to each other, sometimes climbing over one another to get to a nipple.

Social signals such as tail wagging become more important as puppies grow, because tail wagging signals that physical contact and closeness is not threatening. Tail wagging is a signal pups learn starting at about four to six weeks, as soon as they become more active and socially interactive. This signal, along with lowered ears and licking, is usually used as an appeasement signal around food or to solicit food from the parent dog. Some mothers regurgitate food for their puppies, but this seems to happen less and less in domestic situations. Tail wagging and other social signals are also used during play to appease if a play bite was too hard or if play becomes too rough.

By the time she is eight weeks old, your puppy's brain will have grown to five times its original size and will keep growing until she is about a year old. It's during this sensitive time that your puppy might experience her first fear period.

FEAR PERIOD (EIGHT TO TEN WEEKS)

Puppies are not born social animals and are not instinctively welcoming or confident around humans, strange dogs, and other animals—so they learn to bond with others through early positive experiences. This is called socialization. If puppies and dogs are exposed to different environments and social stimuli in a positive way, it helps promote confidence. The sensitive time for socialization is at approximately four to twelve weeks of age, and puppies between the ages of eight and ten weeks often experience what is known as the fear period. Any negative life experiences that occur during this period can have a lasting impression for the rest of the dog's life. This is one of the many reasons why puppies bred in puppy mills and sold over the internet or in pet stores tend to have so many behavioral issues as adults. Puppy mill pups are reared in socially deprived, stressful environments with limited handling by humans. They are prematurely separated from their mothers and then endure traumatic transportation to the pet store, where they are handled by numerous strange people during the time when positive social experiences are crucial.

JUVENILE PERIOD (TWELVE WEEKS TO SEXUAL MATURITY)

By twelve weeks, the puppy is usually in his new home and away from other dogs unless there are dogs in the home. If the puppy is an only dog, it's important to expose him to other puppies and adult dogs while monitoring their interactions to ensure the pup has good experiences.

Sexual maturity usually occurs between six and eighteen months of age, but varies between breeds. Some females start their estrus (cycle) as early as five months old but don't become socially mature until eighteen months to two years old.

Enrichment and Brain Development

Your puppy has already experienced many growth changes by the time you meet her. She might only be two to three months old, but she has already lived a lifetime, and this first part of development has already played a significant part in her appearance, temperament, and behavior. This is because her brain has been molded by her early experiences, and the more enriching, positive experiences she has in those first critical weeks and as she grows, the more her brain has the chance to grow and develop. A puppy might have all her brain cells at birth, but experiences connect them. Puppies that are born and raised in enriching environments have heavier brains than those raised with little enrichment.[5]

Puppies that are raised in nurturing environments from birth are also going to be more prepared and able to cope with novelty in all kinds of situations than puppies that are raised in unstimulating or isolating situations. Early nurturing is critical in building connections between neurons in the brain, which in turn build resilience. Scientific studies have found that deficiencies in early development can have adverse effects on a dog's behavior and disposition in later life.[6] Puppies are more emotionally resilient when they remain with their mothers until seven to eight weeks old, while puppies taken away from their mothers too soon are more likely to be fearful, hyperactive, or even fear-aggressive. It is a testament to a puppy's resilience that they can successfully adapt to new situations or environments even when they haven't had the best start in life.

Picking Your Puppy

The most important questions you should ask yourself before falling in love with a puppy are these: Can you provide everything that a puppy needs, and will he be happy living with you? Think about the kind of questions a prospective pup would ask you if he could interview you before coming into your home. What would you say to him that would prove your worth as a person or family to live with? One of the biggest mistakes a prospective dog owner can make is choosing a puppy based on appearance. A herding breed like an Australian shepherd, for example, may not be the best pet for a couch potato, just as a greyhound may not be a good match for a home with cats. Your commitment level and lifestyle should be taken into consideration, as well as how any animals already in your home might cope with the new arrival.

Dogs can also be costly. The expenses of responsible dog ownership go far beyond the basics of food, water, and shelter. A happy and healthy dog should receive routine veterinary care, a high-quality diet, and regular exercise and mental stimulation. Small expenses like a collar, tag, and dog bed can really start to add up. Even if the decision to bring a puppy into the home is a purely personal one, it has to be a decision accepted by the whole family.

The best age to get a puppy is at about eight weeks old, but this can vary slightly depending on how fast a puppy develops. Some breeders like to hold onto their pups until twelve weeks old, while others take each pup's maturity into account and release them to homes when that pup is ready.

The best time to bring a new puppy or dog into your home is when at least one member of your family has time to spend with him during the adjustment period—two weeks if possible. Once you get your puppy home, let him investigate, explore, and experience his new surroundings, giving him plenty of attention while also giving him the space he needs to adjust to his new home. Gradually exposing your pup to being away from you for short periods of time teaches him to cope better when he is alone.

WHAT BREED IS RIGHT FOR ME?

Your pup's breed is not her destiny. Each dog is an individual—a study of one. Even in highly controlled modern breeds, there are variations in both appearance and behavior. That said, scent hounds do tend to notice their noses more, and retrievers generally learn to retrieve more easily.

Different breeds may also vary in their typical development, and onset of certain instincts also varies by breed. Some dogs don't develop hunting behaviors until after their early socialization window closes, so they are unlikely to hunt any animal they are exposed to and socialized with before the window closes. An Anatolian shepherd that is raised with goats, for example, will not show predatory behavior toward the goats he is protecting, but might chase, kill, and eat rabbits or other small animals. Livestock guarding breeds generally develop very few predatory behaviors.

There are several major breed types that have evolved over time as humans have chosen them for their useful traits. This is known as artificial selection. Artificial selection may not have been conscious and intentional to begin with and probably did not involve any kind of selective breeding. It likely came about as people fed dogs that performed better, which in turn increased the odds of these dogs reproducing, even if the reproduction was not controlled. People may also have favored dogs of a certain appearance regardless of their working success.

These are the major breed types:

- ❧ Sight hounds are majestic sprinters that were bred for speed and to chase prey by sight. They are very useful to hunters as they can see small movements from much greater distances than humans can. Their tendency to chase small things that run fast might not be the best attribute if you have other small animals of any species, but many dogs within this breed type live successfully with cats and other animals. Examples include greyhounds, Irish wolfhounds, borzois, Italian greyhounds, and salukis.

- ❧ Livestock guardians are invaluable for protecting human crops and livestock. They tend to be "one person" dogs in that they are not usually socially gregarious. Examples include Anatolian shepherds, Great Pyrenees, komondors, and Old English sheepdogs.

- ❧ Herders are used to herd livestock in collaboration with humans. These dogs usually have heightened sensory awareness and are able to hear sounds over great distances, which is important when they are working. They like to stalk and chase, which is perfect for herding sheep, cattle, and other livestock. Examples include border collies, German shepherds, Belgian shepherds, and corgis.

- ❧ Every dog has an incredible nose, but scent hounds are the scenting superheroes of the dog world. They are in the hound class, but they tend to be more ground scenters than sight hounds and use a combination of ground and air scenting to find prey. This ability has been harnessed by humans to quickly find things we can't, such as missing articles or people. Examples include beagles, bloodhounds, Rhodesian ridgebacks, and dachshunds.

* Lap dogs and toy breeds are valued for their small size and tameness. They fulfill many jobs, from killing vermin to simply being human companions. Examples include Chihuahuas, bichons frises, Cavalier King Charles spaniels, and Pomeranians.

* Terriers are vermin hunters and can work above and below ground. These dogs are excellent hunters and full of energy. Examples include Manchester terriers, Norfolk terriers, Parson Jack Russell terriers, and Scottish terriers.

* Gundogs find and retrieve game such as birds and other small prey for the hunter. They are strong and agile, able to cover long distances, and use sight and smell to track and find prey. Examples include Labradors, golden retrievers, pointers, and spaniels.

* Working group dogs tend to be large and very strong. They were initially bred to pull heavy loads for humans and are also known as cart or sled dogs. Examples include mastiffs, boxers, Dobermans, rottweilers, and giant schnauzers.

When we say an individual has a personality, we mustn't forget that even though an average personality label can be reliable and consistent, it also includes variation. This variation takes into account environment, experience, and age-related changes. We might be in a place that changes our behavior depending on the social environment we are in, and as we age, our response to things will also change.

What do we mean when we say we want our puppies to be "friendly" or "outgoing"? When we put these labels on our dogs, we expect them to "behave" and to be true to that label in every environment and situation. We forget the simple fact that our behavior changes depending on where we are and who we are with, and the same is true for our dogs.

I am a mixture of labels. I can be an extrovert when I'm teaching a class of students or when I'm doing my live shows to a thousand people in a theater, but I'm an introvert when I'm at a cocktail party and have to make small talk with people I don't know. I am a quiet, compassionate person, but when I see injustice, I will fight for the vulnerable.

You will see personality changes in your puppy as she grows. Some of these changes will be positive and others might concern you, but always look at what influences behavior. If you like it, you can give your pup more opportunities in that situation, but if you don't, avoid those situations so that you keep that variable positive.

Every puppy is different. Her personality is a product of nature and nurture, influenced by specific breed traits. Every individual has a personality that varies as the pup ages, but even if aging and other factors cause changes in behavior, the adult dog will always retain a reliable baseline personality throughout her life.

PUPPY MILLS AND PET STORES

Puppy mills breed pups for bulk and profit with no concern for their health or temperament. Many puppies sold from these places have severe health conditions, and those that do not die within a few weeks of purchase can experience health problems throughout their lives. The financial cost to families is overwhelming, and many puppy mill pups end up being euthanized or dumped into the shelter system.

There is no genetic screening when breeding pups in these facilities and virtually no or limited veterinary care. There are many documented cases of puppies being sold with serious diseases that can also be transferred to humans. These include intestinal parasites such as giardia and less common species of coccidia. Children are at particular risk if they come in contact with such diseases. Parvovirus, canine brucellosis, and canine distemper virus are also common diseases that kill puppies in puppy farms.

Life for the inhabitants of these facilities is very stressful, and stress decreases the immune system, which makes the dogs more susceptible to disease. Confinement and overcrowding allow disease to spread quickly, and dirty food and water harbor microorganisms that also sicken animals. Wire flooring causes injuries that are rarely treated. I have assisted with many puppy mill rescues, and the breeding dogs usually have terrible skin conditions, rotten teeth, ingrown toenails, eye infections, respiratory infections, mastitis, and fleas.

While pups and adult dogs suffer physically, the emotional damage of living in such an environment can also last a lifetime. Puppies have little contact or experience with other dogs, people, or environments in the vital weeks when mental and physical development is so crucial. These puppies are removed from their mothers and sold too young (four to seven weeks old) to maximize profits. It is vital that puppies are with their mothers and their littermates until at least eight weeks old because they learn a lot about social interaction from their littermates and valuable life lessons from their mothers.

Breeding females are used as breeding machines and kept in horrific conditions their entire lives. Most females never see the light of day or feel grass under their feet. Some are so sick that they are unable to give the guidance their puppies need. Studies show that prenatal maternal stress may induce long-lasting alterations in brain structures and functions of the offspring,[7] and many puppies that come from puppy mills are emotionally numb and don't know how to play with toys, other dogs, or humans. Most of the mothers I see in these places are too exhausted to interact appropriately with their pups.

Male dogs used for breeding are kept in similar conditions. When adult dogs from both sexes are no longer producing puppies, they are often drowned, shot, starved, gassed, or electrocuted. Puppy farmers rarely go to the expense of humane euthanasia. It is very normal to find mass graves near puppy farms filled with pups and adult dogs that have succumbed to illness or outlived their usefulness.

A study published in the *Journal of American Veterinary Medicine* in 2013 shows that puppies purchased from puppy farms show an increased prevalence for behavioral problems as adults.[8] The study, motivated by findings in a 2011 study by the same authors, shows that adult dogs rescued from commercial breeding facilities tend to have more psychological problems than pet dogs raised in enriching home environments and suggests that turbulent early lives of dogs in commercial breeding facilities might be the reason for future stress-related behaviors. The extent of the abnormalities in dogs sourced from large-scale breeders is dramatic. Pups from puppy farms show an increased risk of aggression toward their owners and other dogs as well as a greater chance of escaping, roaming, and running away. They are more likely to be fearful, anxious, and depressed and are less able to cope with challenges and novelty in domestic life. The 2011 study was the first scientific evidence that dogs confined in puppy mills for breeding purposes demonstrated impaired mental health.

Regardless of what impressive-looking breed lineage papers from the pet store might say or what pet store owners tell you, the puppies they sell come from puppy mills or backyard breeders. A recent study from the Humane Society of the United States estimates that 99 percent of the puppies that are sold in pet stores come from puppy mills and backyard breeders. Many of these breeding facilities are licensed by the USDA but not regularly regulated.[9] Puppy farming is a profitable business, and the only way these mills can be put out of business is if there is no demand. This will stop the neglect, abuse, and misery of millions of breeding dogs and puppies in the United States, which is why I recommend you get your puppy from a shelter or a licensed breeder. Just remember—no respectable breeder is going to sell their puppies to a pet store, so please avoid getting your puppy from these places unless they are some of the bigger chain stories that allow rescue partners to use these stores to get their dogs and cats adopted.

SHELTERS

I have spent much of my professional life helping rescue animals and it is my favorite line of work. While I wish there wasn't a need for rescue shelters, most of the dogs I work with in public and private are from rescue situations. Even after everything these dogs have experienced, they are some of the most resilient, intelligent, and courageous dogs I work with.

Dogs need social contact with a familial group to keep them safe and secure. Unfortunately, people often let them down and they find themselves alone and abandoned in shelters where stress levels are often high and long hours are spent in a confined space with little social contact. It's a desperate situation for many shelter dogs, but it's a testament to their incredible resilience that they can cope and come out unscathed on the other side. Some rescue dogs may carry a bit of baggage, but that doesn't stop them from thriving in a new home with a family. There is nothing better than seeing a dog go home with his new family and receiving photos and emails weeks, months, and sometimes years after, showing how happy he is.

I am certainly not against good breeders, but because of the pet overpopulation problem, there are many puppies and dogs in shelters that need homes. I always encourage people to go to shelters first. Shelters have all kinds of puppies, and breed-specific rescues are a great resource if you are looking for a particular breed.

LICENSED BREEDERS

A good licensed breeder is someone who breeds for the love of a certain breed. They are dedicated to improving the health and temperament of their dogs and never sell their puppies to a pet store. They might advertise on the internet but do not have multibreed types. They won't suggest you meet in a parking lot. They won't sell their pups at a flea market. Good breeders show you the pup's parents (or at least the mother) of the puppy you are looking at in the breeder's home. The home should be clean, and all dogs, including the mother, should be healthy and friendly. Good breeders usually focus on one or two breeds of dogs and do not have large numbers of dogs and puppies on their property. They also wait until their puppies are at least eight weeks old before they let them go to their new homes.

Breeders also provide proof of health screening on all their dogs and puppies. Some require that you spay/neuter your puppy at a certain age while others encourage you not to breed your puppy if you decide not to neuter. And lastly, a good breeder is concerned about their dogs' welfare throughout their puppy and adult life and usually requires that you sign a contract stating you will bring the puppy or dog back or help find a new home if you need to rehome the dog for any reason.

Word of mouth and references are also good for finding that perfect pup, so researching and asking people who have purchased dogs from breeders ensures that you are going to the right person.

Abigail Witthauer from Roverchase in Birmingham, Alabama, breeds golden retrievers mostly for service dog work. She has sound advice for people who are thinking of getting a puppy from a breeder. "In my opinion," she says, "the best way to decipher whether a breeder is responsible and ethical is whether they are doing genetic health screenings on their dogs prior to breeding. In this day and age, there is simply no excuse for breeders to not be running a full gamut of genetic health screenings on all of their breeding dogs. We, as breeders, have a moral and ethical responsibility to produce dogs with superior health, longevity, and temperament. If we are unwilling or unable to do this, we simply should not be producing dogs."[10]

She also requires that her puppy buyers take their pups to training school. "As a breeder," she says, "the biggest gift I can give my puppy buyers is the requirement of Puppy Kindergarten. In each and every contract required to purchase one of my puppies, one of the stipulations is that you must attend a Puppy Kindergarten group class from an approved trainer. I do a lot of research into the location that each of my puppies will be entering into and select a trainer or selection of trainers that meet the criteria for science-based, positive-reinforcement training methods and require that each puppy begin attending a socialization and experiences class immediately upon entering their new home. It's such a wonderful way for people to begin their lives with their new family member."

CHAPTER 2

Everything's a First

The arrival of a new puppy is a wonderful, life-changing event, but while you're coping with the changes a new puppy brings into your life, don't forget what the transition is like for her. Everything she experiences is new, and while some puppies adjust very quickly to their new homes, others take a lot longer to settle and feel comfortable. Your puppy will have so many new experiences in the first few weeks that you will need to make sure she doesn't get overwhelmed.

If your puppy comes from an environment where she hasn't been handled enough or had any enrichment or socialization, your focus should be on doing some proactive, positive socialization as soon as possible. Don't wait, because you don't have much time before that precious socialization window closes, but do take care not to expose her to too much at any one time.

Preparation and Safety

Be prepared! Make sure you have the basics before bringing your puppy home. These include items such as food bowls, beds, leashes, crates, food, toys, grooming supplies, and baby gates. As long as you have the basics in order, you can take time to see what additional items you might need as you move forward.

Puppy proof your home much the same as you would do for a baby or young child. Puppies love chewing on wires and eating things they shouldn't, so anything that is left within their reach is fair game.

One effective way to puppy proof your home is to lie down on the ground and look at the world from your puppy's point of view. You might notice wires and other chewable items that could be a problem if your pup has access to them. Keeping him away from temptation helps keep him safe.

Bringing Puppy Home

Remember that everything's a first for your puppy as well as for you. Give your puppy time to decompress and don't overwhelm her with too much attention, visitors, or experiences when she first arrives. Relieve pressure by allowing her to explore your home, inside and out. Be there to give her confidence and praise her quietly whenever she chooses to be close to you or makes the decision to go and explore.

It can take time for your pup to adapt to a new setting and routine, so don't expect too much too soon. If your puppy seems nervous, she might need more time to get used to you and your family. You can facilitate the transition by giving her the choice to approach you and other family members rather than always going into her space. All good things come from you and your family—food, praise, play, and petting—but go at your pup's pace and observe her closely to make sure she is not stressed.

Once your pup is used to you and your family, introduce her to other family members, pets, and friends, but make sure you also do this slowly. Everyone wants to show off a new puppy, but ask guests over separately at first so as not to overwhelm her. The more pleasant experiences she has with other people and the pets you have in your home, the better her transition will be.

Never forget that your home and rules are new and different to what your puppy has previously experienced. Regardless of where she came from, your puppy is going to have to follow a whole new set of guidelines, while you and your family are also learning how to live with her. You might not know too much about her life experience before she came to you, but she may have never walked on carpet, seen children's toys, heard the sound of a vacuum, or been close to another animal species. Allow her to safely explore these different experiences and praise her for being calm and brave enough to investigate new things.

Reward behavior you like right from the start. Remember puppies are learning all the time and not just when you're teaching them, so if you see your pup doing something you like, give her positive feedback, which increases the likelihood she will do it again. Reinforcing behavior you like makes your pup feel good and helps establish that all-important bond.

Some of the more mundane activities for us are the scariest ones to a pup: nail trimming, baths, vet/groomer visits, being touched, or even playing with a toy. None of these events (except medical checkups) are more important than your pup's comfort, so be sure to take your time and contact your local certified positive trainer to help build your pup's confidence so that she can cope with these events.

Make time for exercise and fun activities and ensure the exercise is appropriate for the age and size of your puppy. Puppies need gentle activity, so go at your pup's pace and begin to establish a routine. Puppies thrive on predictability, and establishing a schedule for eating, toileting, and event/crate time and play helps your pup acclimate and learn to trust you.

Be careful not to tire your puppy out in the early weeks. Puppies need plenty of naps and are easily exhausted from taking in so much new information. If your pup has come from a rural area to a town or city, allow her time and space to adjust to a busier environment. A puppy that has limited experiences from birth will find herself meeting countless new faces and seeing new things every day. Introducing her gradually and gently to the new sights and sounds of your neighborhood will allow her to live in her new world with confidence.

INTRODUCING YOUR PUPPY TO AN EXISTING DOG

Introducing a new puppy into a household with an existing dog can be tricky, but most dogs ease into the transition well if given the right guidance from the start. Puppies have a great deal of energy, and even highly social dogs already in the home can find a new puppy frustrating. Make sure you supervise all interactions between your puppy and the existing dog, and intervene before things get out of hand. Respond appropriately to your puppy's distress signals and look out for language that your existing dog is uncomfortable, because the resulting conflict could cause both puppy and dog to display aggressive behavior in an effort to increase social distance.

Peaceful coexistence is the goal and can be achieved in a number of ways, including monitoring both dogs' interactions and reducing situational and environmental stress. Remove any triggers that could create tension, such as food, bones, or toys. This reduces the need to compete, and potential fights can be avoided by being vigilant about the location guarding that commonly occurs in multidog households. Toys and chews should be given to the dogs only when they are separated, and feeding can be done separately so there is no tension at feeding time. If the puppy is naturally inquisitive, he might want to investigate your other dog's food or share the toy he is chewing, and that might not go down well with the other dog. Identifying triggers and minimizing stress for both dogs helps develop a better relationship between them.

If you can, introduce your existing dog to the new puppy outside. Space is very important to dogs, and the more space both puppy and dog have to interact and explore, the better. There are interesting smells to discover outside, and these distractions can offer an outlet, giving both dogs an activity to do once they have been introduced. Keep them on leashes until you are confident that they will interact safely, and once they are comfortable with each other, you can bring them inside. Give your pup time to discover his environment with or without the other dog present.

If your existing dog is uncomfortable with the new arrival, you can create a teaching scenario where the new puppy's presence means good things happen to your existing dog. You can do this by standing in the room with your existing dog and having a friend or family member walk into the room with your puppy. As the puppy is brought into the room, give praise and high-value treats or play a game with your existing dog. Tell your puppy how good he is, too, so both receive positive attention in each other's presence. This exercise can be repeated until the older dog becomes more comfortable around the puppy. Relaxed, fluid body language and a willingness to engage in social contact with the puppy will indicate that the technique has been successful.

Walking the dogs together allows them to have positive experiences in each other's presence. The puppy requires less exercise than your older dog to begin with, but a small walk every day helps increase that bond. Start teaching your pup life skills while giving your existing dog a refresher course so that when both dogs are together they can be guided by your cues.

Management is equally important to maintain calm, and baby gates can be highly effective in giving each dog their space. Occasionally, however, gates have the reverse effect and exacerbate tensions. In this case, your puppy and dog should be put in separate rooms and only allowed to interact when they have a lot of space around them, such as in your backyard under your active supervision. Other stress-relieving tools, such as dog-appeasing pheromone, can be used to give the dogs a sense of calm when they are around each other.

Just like with us humans, there will be occasional quarrels even between the best of friends, but it is essential that you don't subject either your puppy or dog to any situation that could cause them to react negatively to one another. If your existing dog does not adapt to the new puppy in time, rehoming options might have to be explored for your pup, but this can be avoided if you are diligent in applying all teaching and management procedures so that both dog and puppy can live peacefully together in a stress-free environment. Remember, your existing dog won't have had much say in the process of choosing his new friend, so be sensitive to the adjustments he has to make to adapt to the changes in his life that happen when you bring a new puppy into the home.

INTRODUCING YOUR PUPPY TO AN EXISTING CAT

If you are bringing a new puppy into the house with an existing cat, you should allow the cat to retain as much freedom as she had before the new arrival and make sure that there are areas for her to go that are off-limits to the puppy. Puppies tend to be less threatening to cats because of their smaller size, but some cats are quite aggressive when they feel threatened, and you need to ensure that your puppy is also protected. It's inevitable that once there is an encounter, your puppy might experience a few corrective swipes from the cat, so make sure your cat's nails are kept short to avoid injury.

During initial introductions, let your puppy explore her environment and keep your cat in another room behind a door and a baby gate. This ensures there isn't a chance meeting between the two until you are ready. Building a good relationship from the start and supervising initial meetings is key.

Once the puppy has explored part of the house without the cat, put her into another room and allow your cat to explore where the puppy has been. This gives your cat an opportunity to smell the new puppy and get important information about her before they meet.

Once you are ready to have cat and puppy greet, open the door and let them sniff each other through the baby gate. Both your puppy and cat will dictate how long they need before they can physically greet in the same room, but it's usually a good idea to do this exercise for a few days so they get comfortable with each other's presence.

When it's time to have them in the same room, put your pup on a harness and loose leash just in case she decides to chase the cat or you need to remove her quickly. Make sure there are places for your cat to escape to and get up high, such as a cat tree. Both animals will respond much better to each other if they feel safe, so provide a bolt hole, such as a high area for the cat or a crate for the pup. Use plenty of praise for calm greetings and if something does happen, gently separate the two and go back to the previous level where both were comfortable. Gradually build up to the point where you can try another greeting.

Your puppy and cat might not become best friends overnight, but hopefully they will acclimate quickly and accept each other's presence. You will have to manage their behavior with each other for a while, especially the energetic interactions of a rambunctious puppy.

Cat food is delicious to dogs because of its high protein content, and cat poop is also a wonderful delicacy. Make sure that your cat's food is placed where the puppy cannot get to it and that the litter box is in a safe area. If your cat starts to have toileting accidents, move her litter box and make sure it is located in a quiet area away from puppy eyes.

The Right Equipment

One of the first things you will want to do with your pup is to get him used to wearing a collar and being walked on a leash, even if he is still too young to be walked outside. Start teaching him how to walk on a leash in your home and yard before taking him out.

NYLON COLLARS

When you first put a collar on your pup, you might notice that she seems uncomfortable and keeps scratching at her neck. This is a common reaction and will stop once she gets used to wearing a collar. Think about the first time you wore a wristwatch or put a ring on your finger. You were probably very aware of this new sensation to begin with, but after a while you adapted and forgot it was there. The same will happen to your pup as long as the collar she is wearing is comfortable.

HARNESSES

Puppies can be walked on flat nylon buckle collars, but I do prefer harnesses and here's why. Harnesses are altogether safer as they distribute weight evenly around the body, so if your puppy pulls, there is no pressure on his delicate neck. There are many different kinds of harnesses you can use. A harness that has a clip located on the puppy's back where the leash can be attached is a great option for a puppy that doesn't pull on the leash. It takes away the pressure and discomfort of a collar and eliminates coughing and choking. These harnesses work well on puppies, small dogs, and dogs that are not inclined to pull or lunge.

However, the back-clipping harness is not a good idea for a puppy that pulls. These types of harnesses can engage a puppy's opposition reflex, which actually encourages pulling. They also minimize the handler's level of control, making it difficult to walk a reactive or pulling pup.

My Positively No-Pull Harness is a tool that can help eliminate pulling and give you more control. A chest-led harness has a front clip located on the puppy's chest and one by the shoulders, while the Positively No-Pull Harness has three points of contact, two on the chest and one just behind the shoulders for added control. The puppy's center of gravity is located at the chest, so when he pulls, the leash that is attached to the front of the chest-led harness simply turns his body around. I designed it to have three points of contact because three loops help limit pulling more by counteracting the natural movement of the harness. Every harness moves when a dog moves, but some harnesses move too much even when fitted correctly. When a leash is attached to the front chest loop on a regular chest-led harness, the harness can shift and the loop can move from the center of the chest to the side of the chest. Because the loop is no longer right at the center of the chest, the harness can lose that no-pull action because the loop is no longer lying at the dog's center of gravity. With two loops placed in the front, just on either side of the pup's center, you can counteract the natural movement in the harness by attaching the leash to the loop furthest away from you. When the pup pulls, the harness will move a little, moving the loop to the center of the chest, thereby keeping that no-pull action. (For harness and other leash resources, see page 202.)

Any harness you purchase should be fitted correctly. Avoid harnesses that constrict around the body, armpits, or chest or that lie too close to a dog's throat. By law your dog should still wear a collar for identification tags, but there is no need to attach a leash to any collar when using a good, reliable harness that will keep your dog safe and comfortable.

CHOKE AND PRONG COLLARS

Choke and prong (or pinch) collars are still very popular with many dog owners. They are generally made of metal chain material and tighten around a dog's neck when the handler pulls or jerks back on the leash. Aversive trainers often use choke and prong collars to perform "corrections," essentially causing the dog pain anytime she pulls on the leash or "misbehaves." While this type of training may stop the pulling or suppress a particular behavior at that moment, it does nothing to get to the root of the dog's issue and doesn't teach her how to walk correctly either. Leash corrections given on these collars cause pain and exacerbate behavior issues, such as fear and aggression.

Even if used without corrections, choke collars cause discomfort and pain and can injure your dog's neck, head, and spinal cord. If you feel your puppy's neck with your hands and then feel your own neck, you can see how similar they are. The trachea, esophagus, thyroid gland, lymph nodes, jugular vein, muscles, and spinal column are all located in similar places. The only difference between a dog and a human neck is that under the fur, a dog's skin layer is only three to five cells thick, while the top layer of skin in humans is denser, at ten to fifteen cells thick.

The thyroid gland lies at the base of the neck just below the larynx close to where any collar sits. Just one yank can cause injury to a gland that controls many of the body's vital functions. Studies show that the thyroid gland gets severely traumatized whenever a dog pulls on the leash, and becomes inflamed. When this happens, it is "destroyed" by the body's own immune system, which tries to remove the inflamed thyroid cells. The destruction of these cells leads to hypothyroidism, which can cause loss of energy, weight gain, skin problems, hair loss, ear infections, and organ failure.[1]

Choke collars also affect other areas of the body, including the eyes. Another study showed that when force is applied to the neck via a leash and a choke collar, pressure in the eyes is significantly increased. This type of pressure can cause serious injury to puppies or dogs already suffering thin corneas, glaucoma, or eye injuries. The same study was conducted with dogs wearing harnesses, which had no impact on eye pressure when force was applied.[2]

Prong collars function similarly to choke collars except they contain metal spikes on the inside that dig into and "pinch" a dog's neck if she pulls on the leash. Prong collar advocates believe that the "pinch" action mimics the teeth of a mother dog grabbing a puppy's neck during a correction. There is no scientific evidence to back up this claim, and it's unlikely that dogs make a connection between the pinch of a collar and a correction given by a mother's mouth, especially as no canine "mother" is physically present.

Dogs walked on prong collars are also constantly subjected to pain and discomfort, which creates fear, anxiety, and aggression on walks. Dogs that are already reactive on leash can become even more reactive due to frustration from collar discomfort. Puppies walked on choke or prong collars are at risk of serious injury.

A study of four hundred dogs concluded that pulling and jerking on the leash with any collar is harmful to a dog's neck and throat. One of the clearest correlations was between cervical (neck) damage and "jerk and pull"; 91 percent of the dogs that had neck injuries had also been exposed to jerking on the leash by the owner or been allowed to pull hard on the leash for long periods of time.[3]

Dogs can't tell us when they are in pain. They put up with near strangulation because the drive to pull forward sometimes overrides the pain at that moment, but the fallout is serious and long lasting. Even when there is so much proof that choke and prong collars contribute to eye, neck, back, and spinal injuries as well as other issues in dogs, there are many who still believe that if used "correctly" these collars are humane and effective tools. Regardless of your personal definition of "humane," it's hard to argue that if something has the potential to cause such damage, how can it be considered humane or safe? Any device that constricts a neck, be it a human or canine one, is dangerous and has the potential to do real harm. Try applying a small amount of pressure to your neck and experience what a puppy or dog goes through when force is applied to any collar. Stay away from these collars and use a harness instead. Buy a couple of different harnesses so your puppy gets used to wearing different equipment. Changing harnesses every few days also helps prevent any friction and hot spots from developing.

SHOCK COLLARS

"Shock," "remote," or "e-collars" are radio-controlled electronic devices on the dog's collar that deliver a static correction (electric shock) whenever a person activates a handheld device remotely. An electric shock is a physiological reaction caused by electric current passing through the body. Depending on the part of the body to which a shock device is attached, the current moves through muscle, skin, and hair. Any kind of aversive, such as an electric shock, has to be relatively strong to be an effective correction, and this can lead to more shocks if the puppy doesn't obey. Regardless of what shock training advocates say, shock, remote, or e-collars are appalling devices and should not be used on any puppy or adult dog, regardless of age, breed, size, job, or problem behavior.

An electric shock, "tap," "pressure," or whatever words the shock collar companies like to use, is a sensation that is sudden and painful, and studies show that long-term negative behaviors, such as aggression, can happen after just one application.[4]

Shock training is often used on dogs that are deemed aggressive or "red zone," because shock trainers see that aggressive or reactive behavior might stop when a static correction is given. While giving your dog a shock every time he does something you don't like might stop the unwanted behavior for that moment, it does nothing to address why the pup is behaving in this way and doesn't give him a chance to learn something more appropriate or feel more confident being around the something or someone that triggered his behavior and, with it, the shock.

Some devices emit an auditory signal or tone, which is usually heard by the dog before the shock is delivered and is therefore associated with the pain of the shock. Shock collar advocates will tell you that once a dog has made the association between the tone and the shock, you might never have to use the shock again because the tone is enough to stop the dog from misbehaving. However, these advocates miss a glaringly simple rule of learning: because dogs make an association between the tone and the shock, just hearing the tone can make a dog very anxious, because of the painful association.

When a shock is delivered, the pain and discomfort can also be associated with something else. For example, if you walk your puppy along the road and your puppy lunges toward a child to say hello and you give him a corrective shock because you think he is being disobedient or his behavior is unsafe toward the child, what do you think the puppy perceives the correction to be for? Lunging? Maybe the fact that he doesn't lunge at another child again for a moment brings you some relief, but is that because he understands that he shouldn't lunge at a child, or is it because you have taught him that going toward a child is painful so he now associates all children with pain? This is one of the many reasons why so many dogs that are shock collar trained can be very reactive to different stimuli in their environment because they now fear any stimulus associated with the painful experience.

Some dogs are so traumatized after experiencing just one shock that a fear memory is imprinted in the brain forever. It saddens me when I see dogs wearing shock collars because trainers like me are usually called in to repair the damage that has been done by a previous trainer who introduced the device. Some of the pups and dogs I have worked with were so traumatized by their experience of shock at the hands of a "shock jock" that they completely shut down. Many refused to go back into their yards or suffered electrical burns from the collars the shock collar companies claim are "safe and humane." It can take a long time and a whole lot of work to make these puppies and dogs feel safe again.

The "simple solution" that the marketing materials from shock companies provide are, in fact, not as simple as they promise and can cause a whole host of problems.

ELECTRIC FENCES

Your puppy will be much safer if she is kept behind a solid fence and not an electronic "containment" system. While electric fences might keep your puppy inside the boundary for a time, unless she sees something so tempting that she runs through regardless of the shock she receives, the electric fence doesn't keep anything out. Anyone can wander onto your property, which is why thieves love electric fences—dogs and especially puppies are so much easier to steal.

I live in a neighborhood that is full of electric fences because the real estate around me is so open. There are constant messages on our neighborhood message boards asking for help finding a dog that is lost because it has gotten out of the property. The description almost always states that the dog is wearing a shock collar.

Shock collar use for training or fences is still popular because shock collar companies have exceptional marketing materials and promise quick results. Niki Tudge, founder of the Pet Professional Guild, states that "the marketing materials of the electronic fence companies often feature photos and videos of dogs romping on huge, lush green lawns without a care in the world. They promise 'freedom' for your dog, over and over again. We (US folks, in particular) are practically wired to have a positive response to that word. But frankly, is a dog alone in a yard, with an automated electronic shock collar strapped tightly around its neck, really free?"[5]

The promise of a cheaper containment option or a quick fix for a "bad" behavior is very tempting in a quick-fix society, but the shock companies say nothing about the safety aspect or behavioral fallout of dogs that have been trained or contained by shock. You might be able to suppress an undesirable behavior for a moment with a shock, but suppressed behavior is not changed behavior and quick fixes very quickly come unstuck.

Is there anything good about shock collar training? Can it really train dogs effectively or save the lives of aggressive dogs that the shock trainers say positive training can't touch? From everything I have observed and experienced in my career, I say absolutely not because we positive trainers are constantly called in to save the lives of even the most difficult dogs. At the end of the day, you have the power to choose how you want to teach your puppy and your adult dog. If you are thinking of going down the shock route, I hope reading this makes you think again, because if you truly want to build a good relationship with your puppy, stay away from the shock jocks and take the time to bond with your pup without using methods or equipment that intimidate or cause pain and fear. And if you are still unsure, ask your puppy or dog what she would prefer. Ask her if she would rather learn life skills using fun, humane methods or be taught with methods that cause pain and the promise of pain if she doesn't comply. What do you think your puppy's answer will be?

What Your Puppy Wants

How do you know what your puppy wants? Reading this book is a good way to find out, but you should also look at what you expect from your puppy at the same time you are working out what your pup's natural desires are. Once you have done this, you can focus on behaviors that you want your puppy to do.

Humans need safety, security, love, food, water, and companionship. Our dogs have the same biological needs as we do, but how do you find out what your particular puppy wants in addition to those needs? And do any of his needs and desires match yours?

If you asked your puppy to write a list of everything he wanted, what do you think he would ask for? I know Jasmine and Sadie desire very different things.

Sadie's list would go something like this:

* I want lots of food—all the time and whenever I ask for it.

* I want to be with you always. I don't want you to ever go out and leave me alone.

* I want twenty-four-hour petting—don't stop!

* I want to smell everything. I love sniffing and want to do that all the time.

* I don't want you to walk me on a leash.

* I want chews, puzzle games, and lots of food-laden toys.

* I want Jasmine to stop humping me when I'm chewing on a bone.

Jasmine's list would go something like this:

* I'm not concerned about food, but I love food in toys.

* I want to sit up high.

* I want to chase every chipmunk and squirrel I see, all the time.

* I don't want strange people touching me.

* I want to play fetch with you more.

* I want you to tell Sadie to stop chewing up my toys.

* I want to roll in smelly poop without you bathing me afterward.

Now make a list of everything you think your puppy needs and wants and then write down everything you need and want from your puppy. See if any of your lists match.

Here's an example of what I need and want from Jasmine and Sadie:

* I need love and companionship.

* I want to have fun and play.

* I want my dogs to be good walking and exercise partners.

* I don't want my dogs rolling in smelly stuff.

- I want confident dogs that can be left alone for short periods of time without chewing or toileting in the house.

- I don't want my dogs biting anyone, and I need them to freely accept anyone I let into my house.

- I want my dogs to be friendly.

As you can see, we ask a lot from our puppies and dogs, and sometimes we don't realize the pressure we put on them to be perfect. We don't want our furniture to be chewed on, our shoes to be eaten, or for them to beg while we are eating; but chewing is a puppy's favorite pastime, and dogs spend most of their lives being hungry. Puppies in particular don't know that they can't toilet in the home unless they're taught. Eliminating outside comes with all kinds of dangers and discomforts, especially when they have to poop in the rain or when the ground is burning from the hot sun.

I often see people running in my neighborhood with panting dogs trailing on the leash behind them, but did they ask if their dog likes running or did they make sure that their dog had the stamina to run with them before they started? A dog's pace is very different from ours, and running slower or trying to keep up with a person if the dog is very small is uncomfortable. I bet they didn't ask if their dog wanted to run with them even if they had the best intentions to give their dog beneficial exercise.

So while there are similarities in what both dogs and people need and want, we do want very different things. Unless we negotiate from both perspectives, we are likely to have problems. To avoid any issues, start thinking about your pup's needs and wants right from the start and be sensitive to what he is trying to tell you. We don't need dogs to survive and be happy, but domestic dogs need our care so they can be safe and survive, and sometimes they have to negotiate tricky waters to do that.

Building a Bond

The human-animal bond describes the emotional attachment between a person and their pet. This bond is further strengthened by feelings of affection and a desire to care for and protect that pet.

It's really quite remarkable that we have a bond with dogs at all considering that we are two very powerful predatory species. The fact that humans and dogs can live together in relative harmony is a testament to the amazing abilities of both species to adapt. Survival depends on how a species adjusts to a changing environment or situation, and dogs have adapted for centuries as they have evolved with us. Dogs share a common ancestor—the gray wolf—and wolves are neophobic (they do not cope well with novelty). They are incredibly shy animals and don't want human contact. Until the invention of modern transport, it was very difficult to study wolves in the wild.

Domestic dogs have evolved to cope with novelty. The dog in your home adjusts to novel things every day—a new person coming into your home, a strange dog on the street, different sights and sounds on a walk or in the car. Most dogs live very successfully in a human domestic environment, and people have encouraged their adaptive skills through selective breeding. We have bred dogs not only to look and behave in a certain way. We have also created a species that has genuine feelings of affection toward us.

Attachment theory has shown that humans have a lifelong need for close affectional bonds with each other. Dogs are like humans in that their need for attachment means that they are also affected by separation and loss. The bond between dogs and people can be as strong as those between a parent and a child.

Evidence of social bonding with our dogs is very obvious. We call dogs our children and refer to ourselves as mom and dad. We celebrate our dogs' birthdays and buy them presents. We spend thousands of dollars a year on food, supplies, clothes, and services.

This is the way we show love to our dogs, but the human-animal bond is not new. In fact, archaeological and anthropological evidence indicates that our bond with dogs has existed throughout our history.[6]

Oxytocin, or the "love hormone," facilitates social bonding. When a mother holds her newborn baby for the first time, oxytocin is released into her body, which bonds her to her child. We experience a surge of oxytocin when we fall in love and when our dogs come to greet us at the end of a long working day. One study has shown that when owners petted their dogs, the dogs' oxytocin levels rose after five to twenty-four minutes of being petted, proving that positive social contact is beneficial for both species.[7]

Oxytocin strengthens social memories in the brain, allowing dogs to bond during social interactions as well as to remember the experience. However, this might not always be a positive thing as research also shows that oxytocin can cause emotional pain and is why stressful situations are remembered long past the event, triggering future fear and anxiety. If a social experience is negative or stressful, the hormone activates a part of the brain that intensifies the memory.[8]

Remember that the first few weeks form your pup's impression of you for the rest of her life, so how you behave will influence how she responds toward you. Building a bond with your puppy is more important to begin with than teaching her cues such as "sit," "come," and "stay," because the relationship you form with your pup at the beginning of her life with you creates a solid foundation for everything else in your future together. If your puppy is playful, play the games she loves. Similarly, if she loves smelling things, take her out to walk and sniff. The more your puppy connects you with pleasant, fun things, the more she'll want to be with you and the more quickly she'll learn when you start teaching her life skills.

Giving Your Puppy Choices

Dog trainers can sometimes overwhelm their puppies and adult dogs with so much "training" that their dogs lose the ability to think for themselves, relying completely on people to direct them. These naturally independent problem solvers are being overtrained and turned into dependent pets. The positive community is more advanced than the traditional one when it comes to observing and listening to what their dogs are trying to say, but there is still a great deal of change needed in the positive community to "do less." The focus must shift away from more structured training to developing dogs' natural social skills and problem-solving abilities.

I have evolved as a trainer and am always open to trying new techniques and ideas because being open to change makes me better. I now work much more organically to give dogs the power they need to deal with situations they find overwhelming or frightening as well as the confidence to make their own decisions. I have seen remarkable changes when clients do less, because the more their dogs have to problem solve and do things for themselves without human interference, the more confident they become.

Giving power back to puppies and adult dogs while providing a guiding hand not only helps them learn new things quickly, but also allows them to adapt to novel situations and environments much more successfully. Relying less on cues and allowing pups to learn what works in certain situations promotes confidence. Gentle guidance helps puppies become more socially adept and emotionally balanced. It isn't in our nature to give up control so easily, but maintaining a good balance of independent and dependent learning makes a significant difference in the lives of our puppies and our adult dogs. For more on the power of giving your puppy choices, see chapter 4, Empowering Your Puppy.

The Loud Puppy

Dogs, like humans, express their emotions by vocalizing, including whining, growling, and barking. It's very common for young puppies to whine and cry as they adjust to new situations, but the first couple of nights with you can be very unsettling to a little one, so setting up a crate or enclosed area next to your bed or having your pup sleep in bed with you will reassure him that he is not alone. Be ready for a few sleepless nights as you both figure out your schedule. Puppy nighttime toilet outings are exhausting, but these gradually decrease as your pup gains more control and begins sleeping through the night. Once this happens on a regular basis, the crate or enclosed area can be moved further away from your bed toward a permanent sleeping area if that is what you prefer.

Anyone who has ever raised a puppy knows what it's like to have sleepless nights. It's inevitable that, at least to begin with, some puppies have a hard time adjusting to a new home and vocalize their discomfort and loneliness. While this is very normal, it is less common for adult and senior dogs to bark at night and even more so if the behavior starts without any known trigger.

When a puppy is with his mom and siblings, his basic needs for food, warmth, and comfort are met. He can choose when to eat, eliminate, and play with his siblings, but when he comes to you, he not only loses the comfort of his canine family, he has to fit into a completely new environment and schedule. It's understandable that this transition sometimes causes anxiety and confusion, and it's one of the main reasons puppies vocalize at night.

Even today, new puppy owners are often told to ignore their pup's whining and only give attention when their puppy is quiet. This technique works with some pups, but the potential for fallout is great. There isn't much research on the effects of controlled crying in puppies, but there has been research into controlled crying in infants.

Controlled crying involves leaving an infant to cry for increasingly longer periods of time before providing comfort. The period of time, rather than the infant's distress level, is used to determine when to attend to the infant or toddler. The aim of controlled crying is to teach babies to settle themselves to sleep and to stop them from crying or calling out during the night.

According to the Australian Association for Infant Mental Health, controlled crying is a "signal of distress or discomfort from an infant or young child to let the caregiver know that they need help. From an evolutionary perspective, crying promotes proximity to the primary caregiver, in the interest of survival and the development of social bonds."[9] While some research suggests that controlled crying works, other studies demonstrate that controlled crying actually raises cortisol levels in an infant's brain.[10]

Responsive parenting, in addition to holding and soothing the baby, helps the baby develop a sense of security and a secure attachment. To deny reassurance during these times can be distressing and may have a negative psychological impact. Research has shown that too much stress is harmful to infants, but every child is different so it's hard to measure just how much is too much.[11]

Because puppies are similar to babies in terms of brain development, it stands to reason that holding and soothing the puppy when he cries helps him feel safe and secure. Studies have shown that giving a puppy what he needs when he asks for it leads to greater independence, greater exploration, and greater confidence when he's left alone.[12]

Having your puppy sleep with you gives him warmth and comfort. If you don't want your puppy to sleep in your bed, put his crate or bed next to yours so you can reach a reassuring hand down to show him that he is not alone. You can put a warm, cuddly toy in his bed so that he has something to cuddle up next to just as he did when he was with his littermates. If your puppy continues to cry, he could be hungry, need to toilet, or have some medical issue that should be addressed.

When puppies get older, they tend to find their own sleeping places and are more resilient to change. If you don't want your puppy to sleep in or next to your bed, transition him to his new sleeping quarters slowly and give him the choice of comfortable sleeping places.

If you have an adult dog or senior dog that is whining and barking at night, this could be because he is nervous, is responding to a noise in his environment, feels unwell, or is having problems with his awake and sleep cycles. Senior dogs suffering with canine cognitive dysfunction ("doggy dementia") often have disturbed sleep cycles and become restless and vocal at night. If your dog is experiencing any of these behaviors, it's important to take him to the veterinarian or veterinary behaviorist before you seek help from a certified positive trainer.

All this can be avoided if the puppy's needs are met right from the beginning. It's much better to prevent your puppy's distress in the first place than to have to deal with it because there is a need that hasn't been met.

Exercise and mental enrichment can significantly reduce nighttime whining and barking as can giving your pup plenty of opportunities to toilet throughout the day. Never use punishment or intimidation to stop your pup from expressing himself as this just serves to increase anxiety and make the behavior worse. The key to reducing nighttime vocalization is to make sure all your pup's wants and needs are being met throughout the day, regardless of why the behavior is occurring.

The Healthy Puppy

Good physical and mental health starts with a visit to your veterinarian. Many dogs build up an aversion to the vet because their first meeting as a puppy is often for vaccinations, which can be painful and overwhelming. One bad experience can set up a lifetime of fear, so once your new puppy is settled in your home, take her to the vet hospital and make sure lots of wonderful things happen to her when she gets there. Take her favorite food or toys with you and have some of the staff feed or play with her. It's an added bonus if you can interact with your vet briefly while you are there, but even if you can't, have a fun visit without checkups or injections. Many trainers will do puppy play or training classes in the vet hospital's lobby, ensuring the puppies have fun experiences in a hospital environment.

Talk to your vet about a health and wellness protocol for your puppy, including a vaccination schedule and wellness checkups. Some vets insist that after all vaccinations have been completed, their clients should have wellness visits every six months or once a year.

VACCINATIONS

Vaccinating your puppy is a vital part of responsible pet ownership. A young puppy's infant immune system is especially prone to illness and disease, so getting your puppy on a vaccination regimen is crucial to having a healthy, happy pet. Questions about when and how to vaccinate and what to vaccinate for are a source of much ongoing discussion, and as veterinary medicine evolves, so too does the need to stay informed:

In a recent blog, Jean Dodds, DVM, estimates that "only about 40 percent of veterinarians are following the current vaccine policy guidelines. There is no such thing as an 'up to date' or 'due' vaccination. Enlightened veterinarians now can offer a package of separated vaccine components, when available, rather than give them all together, since the published data show more adverse reactions when multiple vaccines are administered at the same time."[13]

WHEN TO VACCINATE

Veterinarians typically recommend that vaccines begin at six weeks of age with a single DAPP injection (distemper, adenovirus, parvovirus, and parainfluenza).

At nine weeks, the DAPP needs a booster and your puppy can get her first Bordetella vaccine, if she needs it. At twelve weeks, your puppy will get a DAPP booster and a rabies vaccine depending on what your state and local ordinances are. If she is frequenting environments where there are many other dogs, a Bordetella booster is needed and a leptospirosis vaccine can be given if she is considered at risk. But these are heavy vaccines, so a break between vaccinations is advised.

At sixteen weeks, your puppy gets her last DAPP vaccine and a rabies vaccine if she did not have one at twelve weeks. She also gets a leptospirosis booster if she got the vaccine previously, but again these are strong vaccines and need to be given apart from each other per your veterinarian's advice.

One year from the sixteen-week appointment, the puppy will get her annual exam and vaccine boosters (DAPP, rabies, lepto, and Bordetella). At this time, rabies and DAPP vaccinations can be performed every three years.

Lepto and Bordetella need to remain as a yearly vaccine, and Bordetella may need to be administered every six months, if the dog is considered at risk.

However, vaccine schedules might be changing. According to Dodds, "vaccine experts have recently recommended new protocols for dogs and cats. These include (1) giving the puppy or kitten vaccine series later—starting not before eight weeks of age, except in the cases of outbreaks of virulent viral disease or in orphans or those that never received colostrum from their dams (mothers), followed by a booster at 1 year of age; (2) administering further boosters in a combination vaccine every three years or as split components alternating every other year; until (3) the pet reaches geriatric age, at which time booster vaccination is likely to be unnecessary and can be unsafe for those with aging-related or immunologic disorders."[14]

So what do you do with so much confusing information? It's important that your puppy receive most core vaccines, but you can do more research on the subject and talk with your veterinarian to see what he or she recommends. If the vet says that your puppy should receive all the core vaccines at the same time, you might want to ask about spacing them out or get a second opinion from another vet. Multivaccines can be very tough on your pup's body, especially stronger vaccines for rabies and leptospirosis.

CORE VACCINES

Core vaccines are needed and some are specified by law, including the rabies vaccine. I have broken them down here so that it is clear what they do and why they are needed.

RABIES

The rabies vaccine is required by law in all states in the United States. Rabies is a devastating virus that is frequently carried by wildlife and can be transferred to your pet through saliva and other secretions. Rabies is a zoonotic disease (that is, it can be transmitted to humans) and can be fatal if not treated quickly. It is important to keep your pet up to date on the rabies vaccine and to know state laws for your area in the event your dog bites someone or gets bitten by local wildlife.

PARVOVIRUS

Parvovirus is highly contagious among unvaccinated puppies. The virus infects cells of the small intestine, which leads to severe diarrhea, dehydration, and lethargy. Because this virus infects rapidly dividing tissues, it can kill a puppy quickly. The only treatment for parvo is to keep the puppy hydrated with IV fluids.

ADENOVIRUS

Adenovirus causes liver infection in dogs. The virus is easily spread through body fluids and excretions. Symptoms include fever, lethargy, eye discharge, skin bruising, vomiting, and diarrhea.

DISTEMPER

Distemper is closely related to measles in people, but it isn't a zoonotic disease. The virus is spread through the air like a cold. Symptoms include eye and nasal discharge and, if untreated, can lead to pneumonia.

NONCORE VACCINES

Noncore vaccines should be administered on a case-by-case basis. They shouldn't be given at the same time with any other types of vaccines. Think about getting these noncore vaccines if your puppy frequently swims in creeks and other bodies of natural water, goes to day care or boarding kennels, or frequents dog parks and other places where dogs are present.

CANINE INFLUENZA

The flu virus is spread like cold and flu viruses in people but is not a zoonotic disease. Symptoms include lethargy, fever, loss of appetite, nasal discharge, and a cough. You should vaccinate against influenza if your puppy is regularly exposed to other dogs in day care or kennel environments and there is evidence of canine flu in your area.

BORDETELLA

Bordetella is more commonly known as kennel cough and is caused by a secondary bacterial infection with Bordetella after the dog has been infected with the canine flu virus. This disease is an infectious bronchitis of dogs characterized by a harsh hacking cough that may sound like something is stuck in your dog's throat. Your dog will need this vaccine if he interacts with other dogs in dog parks, day care, or boarding facilities.

LEPTOSPIROSIS

Leptospirosis is a bacteria that is spread through the urine of local wildlife and contaminates water and soil. Once exposed, the organism affects mainly the dog's liver and kidneys. Most dogs are considered at risk, as cases have been reported throughout the United States; local wildlife exposure is extremely hard to prevent. If your dog swims and drinks from creeks and lakes, consider getting this vaccine. Symptoms of the disease are lethargy, fever, increased drinking and urination, and, in some cases, vomiting and diarrhea.

CORONAVIRUS

Coronavirus is a highly contagious disease that is mild if it's the only infection, but your puppy can become very sick if the infection is combined with parvovirus. Symptoms include vomiting and diarrhea.

ARE VACCINATIONS SAFE?

Regardless of the debate in the veterinary community about which vaccines should be administered when, the general consensus is that vaccines, especially puppy vaccines, are vital for your puppy's well-being and for the safety and well-being of the community.

In rare cases, dogs can have adverse reactions to vaccines, called vaccinosis. Some reactions are mild, while others can be potentially life-threatening. If your dog has a reaction to a vaccine, your veterinarian can advise on the best way to keep your dog immunized without subjecting her to unnecessary additional vaccines. You should always monitor your dog for any health or behavior changes immediately following the administration of any vaccine. Prompt intervention can help keep more serious symptoms from developing.

VACCINES AND PUPPY SOCIALIZATION

Can I socialize my puppy with other puppies and dogs before he has all his vaccines? I get asked this question a lot, and, while you should avoid bringing your puppy to areas that are heavily traveled by other dogs (such as pet stores, dog parks, and so on) until he is fully immunized, it is also important that you don't keep your puppy isolated or prevent him from interacting with other dogs. In doing so, you will miss his critical fear periods when it is extremely important for your pup to have positive experiences.

Find a certified positive trainer who holds puppy classes. These classes are specially designed to be fun and safe for your puppy. Make playdates in your home or yard with immunized dogs you know. Invite friends and family over to help socialize your puppy and make sure they wash their hands before touching him. Take your puppy for rides in the car so that he can experience the larger world around him, making sure that the car is a safe place and a car ride is a pleasant experience for him.

Veterinary behaviorists caution that the risk of developing behavioral problems—especially aggression—outweighs the risk of developing disease in otherwise healthy puppies. As early as 2004, renowned veterinarian R. K. Anderson proclaimed this in an open letter to his veterinary colleagues: "Puppy Vaccination and Early Socialization Should Go Together!"[15]

Lynn Honeckman, DVM, tells us, "There is a very small window of opportunity during which it is our job to teach our puppies that the world is a safe place. After the four- to twelve-week 'critical period' window closes, the friendly socializing puppy that was open to accepting the wide and wonderful world, enters into a fear-acquiring developmental period. So . . . unless you and your dog plan to live in the woods and need to protect yourselves from other dogs, preparing your pup to live in a domesticated, dog-filled environment makes better sense!"[16]

COMMON PARASITES

Parasites can cause serious problems, especially for young puppies, so it is vital that you protect your puppy from these pests right from the start. Do check with your vet about the best medications to use and when to use them so that your puppy is protected but not overloaded with too much strong medication at any one time.

FLEAS

Fleas are probably the most common parasite of dogs and can be a year-round problem. Fleas typically cause one or more of the following problems:

- Mild to severe itching, scratching, biting, and chewing
- Flea saliva hypersensitivity or allergy and resulting skin problems
- Transmission of tapeworms
- Anemia and possible death (most often in very young or small animals)

Fleas can be detected by direct examination. The presence of flea dirt (small black specks of dried flea feces) on the dog also confirms fleas that are usually found around the neck, hindquarters, and above the base of the tail.

TICKS

These creatures can cause signs that range from mild local irritation to severe anemia. In addition, ticks can transmit many other diseases to animals and humans. These diseases include Lyme disease among others. Ticks can be detected by direct examination. Removal is easy with a pair of tweezers, by grabbing the head of the tick with the tweezers and twisting as you pull the tick out, making sure you get the legs as well. Any tick body parts left in the skin can cause infections, so it's important to get the tick out completely.

MITES AND LICE

These are less commonly seen in dogs than fleas and ticks. The two main types of mites include sarcoptic mange and demodectic mange, a condition that often results when a dog is neglected and not given proper veterinary care. Symptoms include itching, hair loss, dandruff, lesions, and bleeding skin. Sarcoptic mange can be transmitted to people.

ENDOPARASITES

These parasites live within dogs and include heartworms, roundworms, hookworms, whipworms, and tapeworms. It is vitally important that your puppy is dewormed regularly and that heartworm prevention medication is given monthly to dogs in infected areas.

Heartworms

Heartworms are transmitted to dogs and cats through the bite of an infected mosquito. Adult heartworms primarily live in the major blood vessels of the heart and lungs. Immature heartworms circulate throughout the blood vessels in the rest of the body. Signs of heartworms can be vague and hard to detect until late in the course of the disease. They include coughing, difficulty breathing, panting, exercise intolerance, decreased activity level, and sudden death. Heartworms can be easily detected through a yearly blood test in areas where the likelihood of getting heartworms is high, such as the southern United States.

Roundworms, Hookworms, and Whipworms

Roundworms, hookworms, and whipworms are among the most common internal parasites. These parasites live within the gastrointestinal tract of dogs and can cause diarrhea, anemia, loss of body condition, and so on. These parasites can be easily detected by testing a puppy's poop.

Tapeworms

Tapeworms are another example of a gastrointestinal parasite. Tapeworms can also cause diarrhea, weight loss and poor body condition. Fleas can carry and transmit tapeworms to dogs or they can be transmitted by rodents and rabbits.

COMMON INFECTIONS

Puppies are also susceptible to infections. Here are the more common infections you need to look for.

EAR INFECTION

An ear infection can come on without warning and can be characterized by excessive scratching at the ears and head shaking. There is often a bad odor coming from the ears, which can be red and inflamed, and if the infection is chronic, the external part of the ear may become thickened and irregular.

If your puppy has recurrent ear infections, the vet will investigate if an underlying cause, such as allergies, should be investigated. For dogs prone to ear infections, cleaning the ears with a veterinarian-approved product after swimming or bathing can help reduce the risk of an ear infection.

URINARY TRACT INFECTION

If you are having a hard time toilet training your puppy or notice that your toilet-trained pup is having accidents again, she might have a urinary tract infection. This infection is characterized by frequent urination, inappropriate elimination, and blood in the urine. A urinalysis needs to be evaluated by a veterinarian to confirm the presence of the infection and ensure there are no urine crystals (solidified chemicals in urine that often accompany infection).

PUPPY PYODERMA

Puppy pyoderma generally occurs in puppies eight to ten weeks old and is characterized by skin lesions that are red. They are most commonly found on the belly, armpits, and groin areas of the puppy but can occur anywhere. The lesions are not painful and are rarely itchy. Antibiotics are often prescribed for this disease.

HOT SPOTS

Hot spots (also known as acute moist dermatitis) are very common. If you live in a part of the country where humidity is high or your pup has an allergy to fleas, this condition can flare up very quickly. Symptoms include itchy skin and lesions that can quickly become infected when licked or scratched.

ANAL SAC ISSUES

Anal sacs are glands on either side of the anus that excrete fluid containing pheromones. When your puppy poops, his anal glands naturally express themselves, but sometimes they can become impacted. If you see your puppy scooting his bottom along the ground or notice a fishy smell coming from his rear end, his anal glands might need to be manually expressed, which can be done by your veterinarian.

Feeding Your Puppy

The dog food industry is a minefield of massive proportions. People feel as strongly about what they feed their dogs as how they train them. Advocates for a completely raw diet don't understand why most of the dog-owning public feed their dog commercial kibble and meat from tins. People who feed their dog kibble don't understand how some people cook "people food" for their dogs. To help you negotiate this minefield, I've answered some universally asked questions that will better guide you to make the right decision for your puppy.

No one size fits all. What might be right for one pup will not be good for another, so take advice and do your research. Ultimately, it comes down to what food your puppy likes, what keeps her healthy, and what you are comfortable feeding her. Your pup is essentially a carnivore with pointy back teeth that are especially designed to chop up meat. Meat is a high-protein food that all puppies need, but from a dietary perspective your pup will also benefit from eating plant-based foods, and most commercial dog food contains both animal and plant ingredients.

COMMERCIAL DOG FOOD

Dogs have been living in close proximity with humans for over ten thousand years, but it's only in the last 150 years or so that dog food was introduced. This was still a meat-based wet food until the 1950s when there was a drastic change in the way dogs were fed in the United States, with the introduction of a dried food called kibble. The United States produces a large amount of corn, and during the 1950s, there was a surplus of corn production, which went to creating animal feed, including dog food. Dogs began to eat complete diets in the form of heat-dried pellets, and there are now thousands of food products to choose from, ranging from processed kibble to raw, frozen, and freeze dried.

So what constitutes a nutritious diet, and how do you know your puppy is getting the nutrition he needs?

The Association of American Feed Control (AAFCO) does not "police" the pet food industry but establishes nutritional standards for a complete and balanced pet food. It is a pet food company's responsibility to formulate products according to AAFCO standards, which states that the food should be nutritionally complete and balanced.[17]

WHAT MAKES FOOD HEALTHY?

Your growing puppy will need different nutrition at various life stages. Optimum nutrition at any stage demands that protein, fat, carbohydrates, and micronutrients (such as minerals, vitamins, and enzymes) are in balance with each other. Whatever you decide to feed your dog, the food should be palatable and help your puppy maintain proper weight with strong bones, clear eyes with good vision, a smooth and dander-free coat, and a consistent stool.

It is generally recommended that whole meat protein should be the first ingredient listed on the package and that there should be limited meal and by-products in the food. Artificial colors and preservatives should be avoided.

A by-product is a part of the animal that is not normally intended for human consumption. This includes the lungs, spleen, kidneys, brain, liver, blood, bone, stomachs, and intestines of meat animals, and the necks, feet, undeveloped eggs, and intestines from poultry. By-products should not include hair, horns, teeth, or hooves.

GRAIN-FREE DOG FOOD

Grain-free kibble and canned food have become extremely popular in recent years, but there is now concern that grain-free diets might be causing heart disease in some dogs. The condition is dilated cardiomyopathy (DCM), in which the heart weakens and becomes enlarged. Symptoms include fatigue, difficulty breathing, coughing, and fainting. Some dogs can abruptly go into heart failure.

DCM is typically seen in large-breed dogs that have a genetic predisposition for it, like Doberman pinschers, Irish wolfhounds, boxers, and Great Danes. But recently a practice of nineteen veterinary cardiologists in the Baltimore–Washington, DC, area alerted the FDA that it has been seeing DCM among other breeds, including golden retrievers, doodle mixes, Labrador retrievers, and shih tzus. The common factor was a diet heavy in peas, lentils, chickpeas, and potatoes—carbohydrates typically intended to replace grains.

Lisa Freeman, a veterinary nutritionist and researcher with the Cummings School of Veterinary Medicine at Tufts University, is skeptical about grain-free diets. She states that, "contrary to advertising and popular belief, there is no research to demonstrate that grain-free diets offer any health benefits over diets that contain grains. Grains are an important source of protein and other nutrients in many meat-based pet foods and have not been linked to any health problems except in the rare situation when a pet has an allergy to a specific grain."[18]

IS CORN BAD FOR YOUR PUPPY?

Corn has been used as a filler in dog food since the 1950s. It is known as a hot grain and can cause gastrointestinal upset and allergies. Other grains are said to cause allergies, but studies have found that more common allergies might be the result of feeding a dog dairy- or beef-based foods. We found out very quickly that my Sadie was allergic to chicken because eating it made her itchy and caused flaky skin and hot spots. She suffers from an overproduction of yeast and allergies that make her lick her paws until they are red raw. As soon as we changed her diet, her food allergies and yeast production disappeared.

Whatever you decide to feed your puppy, observe him closely to make sure he is tolerating the food you have chosen for him.

Pay attention to the ingredient list and the nutritional value of ingredients. Appropriate amounts of precisely formulated nutrients are just as important as ingredients, and no single ingredient provides the best protein balance for pets; the best balance comes from a combination of ingredients.

If your puppy is eating too many carbohydrates and has limited opportunities to exert extra energy, he may become irritable and destructive. Working dogs that expend a lot of energy usually require a diet that is higher in protein, but too much protein or not enough carbs might not be good. A dog that is not satiated can show neurotic behaviors during the day and in between meals because of an unstable level of glucose and insulin concentration in the blood.

You are what you eat, and that's true for your puppy too. Feeding him a good diet will keep him healthy and fit, but food also has a powerful effect on behavior. A healthy, nutritious diet is essential for a happy puppy, but if you see a physical or emotional change, consider what you are feeding him and consult your veterinarian immediately.

HOW DO I FEED MY PUPPY?

Every puppy has different nutritional needs depending on her breed, activity level, or the environment she lives in. Because puppies grow quickly, they need sufficient calories to keep up with their rapid growth process, so having access to plenty of good food is important.

I don't recommend free feeding—that, is leaving the food out all day for the puppy to eat at will. This might cause health concerns, especially if she eats everything in one go. It also limits trainability as she becomes satiated and has no interest in food rewards, and it can make toilet training harder, as there is no feeding/elimination schedule. Some dogs are good at regulating what they eat, but others will consume whatever you put in front of them, particularly dogs that live in multidog households. If your puppy is a picky eater and leaves her food, chances are another dog will eat it up and she won't get the calories she needs.

Regulated feeding is better. In general, puppies up to six months of age require two to three meals a day. I don't recommend feeding an adult dog once a day because dogs get hungry, especially if they have a fast metabolism, and leaving a stomach empty for twenty-four hours can cause changes in energy, mood swings, and medical problems such as hypoglycemia, especially in small dogs. Feeding your puppy on a regular schedule will help you get a better idea when your puppy is most likely to toilet and helps with toilet training.

FEEDING TIME MAYHEM

When you share your life with a dog, mealtimes can be a little chaotic. Whether you live in a multidog household where food is a trigger point for disagreements or you have a chow hound that inhales his entire bowl in a single bite, there are some things you can do to help make mealtimes a little calmer.

Feeding time in a multidog household can get out of control, especially when you have dogs that really love to eat and a puppy that loves investigating. Don't let your puppy learn the hard way! The key to reducing chaos is to establish a consistent routine that allows your puppy and each dog to eat separately and in peace. You may find your dogs eat more slowly and confidently if they don't feel that food will be stolen from them.

With this in mind, try feeding each dog in a separate crate (with the doors closed so nobody can sneak into the other's crate). This is an easy, hassle-free solution to keep dogs away from each other while eating. You can also feed your dogs either in separate rooms or on a rotation where one dog eats while the others are put away. Baby gates might be the best way to help achieve calm around mealtimes.

SLOW DOWN

Don't let your puppy inhale her food, because dogs that have a habit of eating too quickly are susceptible to potentially life-threatening illnesses like bloat. If your puppy is a fast eater, there are many great products on the market designed to help slow her down during meals. From specially designed slow-feeding bowls to timed treat and food dispensers, these devices help your puppy eat at a slower and healthier pace, which will keep her safe as she grows.

The dog bowl is a great feeding tool but doesn't make mealtimes fun or interesting. If you always give your puppy her food in a bowl, you're missing out on some easy learning opportunities. Whether you are raising a working dog or just a family companion, you can send her on a scavenger hunt by putting her food in one or multiple interactive toys and hiding them throughout the home. Tell her to go find it and let her use her natural hunting skills to track the food down. Not only will you enrich your pup's life by encouraging seeking behavior, you will also give her plenty of valuable mental and physical stimulation with minimal effort required on your end.

IMPULSE CONTROL AT FEEDING TIME

If you have a puppy that jumps all over you or dives for the bowl during feeding time, teaching a "wait" cue can make a huge difference. This cue teaches your puppy to exercise valuable impulse control around a food source and is relatively easy to teach. Do remember, however, that even though you are teaching your pup to control his impulses around his food bowl, it's not true self-control until the puppy can regulate his own behavior when food is present without your instruction or intervention. We often say that our dogs have good "self-control" when, in reality, the pup only exercises this "control" when we are present.

Here's how you teach the "wait" cue:

- ❧ Hold your pup's empty food bowl and ask him to "wait."

- ❧ Move the food bowl toward the floor a few inches. If your puppy stays in his place, keep lowering the bowl until you can place it on the ground. If he tries to jump up, grab the bowl, or do any other undesirable behavior, simply say "oops!" and bring the bowl back up again.

- ❧ Practice lowering the bowl a few inches at a time and continue rewarding your pup with praise as he waits patiently. Move in small increments so that you set him up for success.

- ❧ Eventually, you should be able to place the bowl on the floor while your puppy waits until you tell him it's okay to eat.

CHEWS AND TREATS

There are hundreds of different brands of chews and treats for puppies and dogs, but how do you know what's safe?

The size of your puppy's mouth will determine the size of the chew you give, but to be as safe as possible, you should only give chews when you are there to actively supervise her. Even if the chew is large, your puppy might chew it down to a point where she could choke on small pieces. Bones are a welcome treat but care needs to be taken. Feeding raw beef bones, for example, are safer than feeding cooked bones, but veterinarians do warn against some bones as they can fracture delicate teeth and cause mouth or jaw injuries. Other bones can cause constipation or obstructions in the esophagus, trachea, stomach, small intestine, colon, or rectum and, in very rare cases, can cause sepsis or peritonitis from complications of obstructions.

Don't give your puppy raw hides, deer antlers, or adult chew toys as these can cause stomach upsets and hurt mouths. Stick to puppy-appropriate toys that are gentle on growing bodies and developing teeth.

CHAPTER 3

Teaching Life Skills

What is a life skill? Like a child, your puppy will need to develop many physical and mental skills in order to navigate through life successfully. Teaching a life skill can be achieved through a specific training technique or game, or it can be learned by an experience that you provide. Throughout this chapter, I discuss different life skills and the steps you can take to teach them.

An important part of the learning process is to set your pup up for success by managing his environment and making it easy for him to do well. This begins with understanding how your pup copes in certain situations. For example, if your puppy is highly social and loves new people coming into your home, teach him to greet without jumping on your guest as they enter. This helps inhibit excitable behavior while still allowing him to enjoy the new person's arrival. However, if your pup is wary or fearful of new people, take pressure off him by putting him behind a baby gate or in his own room as they enter. Space is vitally important for puppies and dogs that are socially inexperienced or fearful, and managing your environment to reduce pressure keeps everyone happy and safe.

Don't forget that your puppy learns from his environment all the time and will naturally gain skills from his experience. We often spend so much time pairing life experiences with something good, like a piece of food or a treat in an effort to build up positive associations, that we often interrupt what can be an easy, natural learning experience.

When I was an actor, I was taught to "do less" and "just be." Amateur actors tend to do too much, which makes their acting unbelievable. But when you stop trying so hard and do less, your delivery becomes more genuine and your performance gets better. I feel the same way about puppy raising and dog training. Your puppy is picking up so much from just living with you that the learning never stops. So much can be done by just putting your puppy into situations where you can ensure success, and, while you might have to intervene at times, a lot can be learned by just being present and letting your puppy discover and experience the environment or situation in his own time and in his own way.

Raising a Resilient Puppy

What is the first thing you want to do when you see a puppy? Do you want to pick her up and hold that warm, wiggly body and kiss that mushy face? I can't think of anyone who doesn't want to interact with a gorgeous bundle of fur, but from the puppy's point of view, too much handling can be uncomfortable.

I am constantly fascinated with just how adaptable puppies are. As I've mentioned, this comes from thousands of years of evolution. Dogs that adapt well to novelty do better at living with humans, and the dogs that function better within human society are the ones that will be successful in the home.

All animals need to feel safe and secure, but they also need a degree of autonomy and predictability. It's very hard to negotiate an ever-changing world when you don't understand what is going on or when you have no power to change it. When you were a child, it was up to your parents to help you become resilient enough not only to understand the world around you, but to live successfully within it even when experiencing stressful situations. The way you help build resilience in a child is very similar to how you build resilience in a puppy.

When a puppy has an experience that causes a temporary fear reaction, the time it takes to recover or bounce back from that experience is called the rate of recovery. Recovery time is an important way to measure resilience. How quickly does it take your puppy to recover from a scary experience? Does she retreat into her shell or does she carry on investigating whatever caused the scary experience? Recovery time is biological and relies on how fast neurons in the brain, especially in the amygdala (the brain's emotional center), can recover. This depends on genetics, early development, and the situation and environment to which your puppy is exposed.

If your puppy hears a loud noise that scares her, she might be unable to cope with hearing it again and her resilience will be low. Even though it can be hard to change your puppy's response to that and similar noises, it's not impossible. Trainers and behaviorists call this process behavior modification. We help puppies and older dogs see things differently by managing the environment around them while using methods and training techniques designed to help pups feel more confident and comfortable in the human domestic world.

MANAGEMENT

You can create a predictable environment by managing your puppy's everyday life. If your puppy is afraid of thunder, for example, you can close the curtains, put on some calming music (see "Canine Noise Phobia Series," page 151), and create a bolt hole he can go to that makes him feel safe. Sometimes your puppy will create his own hiding space by going into the closet or under a bed, and if this is where he feels protected, it's best to create a den for him there and let him be until the thunderstorm passes.

If your puppy gets stressed in your car, he might be getting overstimulated by what is flying past outside the window. In this case you would manage the situation by putting him in a crate and draping a blanket over part of the crate to block his vision and let him relax until you get to your destination.

If your puppy is stressed in the crate, then placing the crate in a puppy-proofed area of your home or in an ex pen so that the crate always stays open will give him the freedom to make decisions about whether he wants to go into the crate or not. Not all pups can tolerate being confined.

PREDICTABILITY

Puppies and adult dogs don't have much choice in their daily lives, and this can lead to insecurity. I will focus more on giving choices to your puppy later in this book, but know that choice and predictability go hand in hand. Our dogs spend most of their day not knowing when anything is going to happen because they don't have the ability to make decisions or fully understand the decisions we make for them.

If you have an unconfident puppy, you can create an environment and situation that is more predictable. A predictable routine manages expectations and gives puppies consistency. Creating a feeding, walking, and play schedule can make a pup feel more secure because she knows what to expect.

Clear communication breeds confidence. Be consistent with your responses and your cues and encourage your family to do the same. When we adopted Jasmine, we noticed how she would cower when we went to pick her up. She didn't have the best start in life and we had to introduce her to everything, including meeting people, seeing a car, and walking on grass. I hated seeing her cower when all we wanted to do was to give her some love, but I stopped reaching out to her and got her comfortable with my touch first before bending over and picking her up. Once she was a little more relaxed, I taught her what I call the "pick up" cue, which is a cue I use to tell her that I'm about to reach down toward her, take her in my arms, and lift her off the ground. She loved being held, so I knew this "life reward" was the reinforcement she needed. After gently practicing this cue, Jasmine began to associate the words "pick up" with being held, and very soon she was offering me her side body and even helped me pick her up by doing a little jump as my hands extended toward her. The "pick up" cue became a reliable and consistent phrase, and the predictability of this cue made her feel more confident and secure.

A puppy can't build resilience if she isn't emotionally stable. Making sure her needs are met is very important, and giving her plenty of opportunities for physical exercise and mental enrichment helps build a healthy body and healthy mind.

THE ADAPTABLE PUPPY

In many cases, a puppy does not sensitize to something or become fearful when a stimulus is repeated. In fact, instead of becoming more fearful as the stimulus recurs, the puppy may start to behave more calmly and eventually even appear to ignore the stimulus. This phenomenon is called habituation.

Habituation is a process that occurs when a stimulus leads to no predictable consequence, so that the puppy learns that the stimulus is essentially irrelevant. It is usually a natural process that doesn't require human interference. Imagine you move to a new house and your yard backs onto a railway line. For the first week you notice every train that goes past, but as days go by, train sounds become less interruptive until eventually you don't even hear them anymore. You have naturally habituated to the noise of the trains.

So habituation works most quickly when a stimulus is repeated several times in a brief period of time. For example, if there is construction nearby, a dog may at first startle at the sound of a jackhammer and then become calmer and calmer as the noise continues—even if the jackhammer starts and stops a few times. The dog might startle again at the sound of the jackhammer on the following day, since what has taken place so far is likely short-term habituation.

Long-term habituation is the process where an animal learns to ignore a stimulus even when it hasn't occurred recently (for example, when a jackhammer unexpectedly starts up). It usually takes many repetitions of the situation before the dog stops responding to the stimulus.

Handling Your Puppy

To avoid handling issues in puppies, pay attention to how you pick a puppy up, how tight you hold him, and how firmly you stroke him. Sometimes a touch that is too light might tickle while stroking too hard might hurt, so always look at how your puppy accepts your touch. Does he stay and ask for more if you stop stroking him or does he walk away? Does he growl at you when you touch him or does he lick your hand? The way he responds to your touch will indicate how he feels. The same is also true for adult dogs.

Getting your puppy used to being touched by you and other people is also really important for when your puppy goes to the vet. If he is used to having his ears looked into and his mouth opened by you and a select few in your home environment, it will be easier for him to accept being touched by another person in the vet's office or at the groomers. You can pair each touch with something positive, like praise or a treat, and not subject your pup to too much handling in the beginning. It's also important to have other people handle him so he gets used to being touched by strangers. This will prevent touch aversion with others as he grows older.

If your puppy growls, snaps, or bites when he is being handled, he might have a touch sensitivity issue, feel pain, or be frustrated because he's being prevented from doing something he wants to do. Take your puppy to the veterinarian to rule out any medical issues he might have, and if he is given a clean bill of health, there might be a more significant behavioral issue to address. Limit the amount of times you handle him and pair handling with something he loves, like a game, toy, or some food. Talk to him and give him plenty of praise until you gradually build up to the point where he is more tolerant, but don't go too fast as this might impede success.

The secret to making grooming or cutting your puppy's toenails easier is to practice grooming or cutting before you actually have to do it for real. Gently introduce your pup to the practice of toenail clipping by touching his paw with your hand, followed by a treat and/or praise. Once he is comfortable with his paws being handled, let him investigate the clippers you are going to use by allowing him to smell them as you hold them in your hand. As soon as he moves his nose to touch the clippers (most dogs will be naturally curious about anything you present to them), mark that action with a "yes" or similar cue word and give him a treat or praise. A pup's paws can be sensitive and handling can be uncomfortable if not ticklish, so be aware of this as you handle him. You can advance to touch the clippers to your puppy's paw and if he accepts that touch, you can advance to cutting one nail, followed by a lot of praise. The more patient you are with this process, the more likely it is that your pup will habituate to having his nails clipped.

Most handling issues can be prevented if puppies are taught to accept and enjoy being touched from an early age, but these habituation processes can also be used for adult dogs in many different situations and for dogs that have become sensitized to handling and need to be taken through a gentle desensitization process. The general rule for success is to go at each puppy's pace, observe body language, and be sensitive to their different learning styles and needs.

Coping with Human Greeting Behavior

How would you respond if a person you didn't know suddenly walked over to you and touched you on the top of your head? You might be shocked at first and maybe say a few choice words, push the person away, or move away from them quickly; but our dogs almost never have that luxury, and when they do communicate how freaked out they are, they are often punished for growling, snapping, or biting. This is what our puppies and adult dogs experience daily from well-meaning people who can't resist making a fuss over the dog walking past them. People want to touch, hold, and hug dogs, and this can be very frightening, especially when they're being touched by a person they don't know.

Some pups have an automatic defense reflex when a hand comes toward them or extends over the head. When a puppy is very young, this reflex is not under conscious control, so it's vital to teach your puppy to accept being touched with an approaching hand.

I like to prepare my pups for "rude" human behavior, including greetings and being held. Of course it's important for puppy parents to make sure this doesn't happen frequently, but the puppy will be prepared if it does. This is one of the most vital social lessons a puppy can learn, because human invasion of space, as well as being touched on the head, will happen many times throughout her life.

Here are some teaching tips to get your pup used to human greeting behavior:

- 🐾 Stand in front of your puppy.

- 🐾 Lean over her and, as you do so, praise her and give her a piece of food.

- Keep repeating this action until your puppy is relaxed with you leaning over her.

- As you lean forward and give her food, take your other hand and pet her on the top of the head. Keep praising her and telling her what a good girl she is.

- Repeat this exercise a few times as long as your pup is comfortable.

- If at any time your puppy looks uncomfortable, stop and go back to the level she was comfortable with and build up again slowly.

- If your puppy accepts this movement, you can gradually increase distance by walking away, turning around, walking toward her, bending down, and touching her on the head.

- Once she accepts this approach, repeat the exercise while talking and smiling at your puppy.

- Add a bit more energy and enthusiasm into your greeting, exactly like a well-meaning person does when greeting your puppy for the first time.

- Once your puppy accepts your approach, practice with other people she knows before asking friends she hasn't met to come say hello.

Training Your Puppy

You can prevent unwanted behaviors by teaching your puppy life skills. Every dog needs to learn how to live successfully in a home environment. Domestic dogs might seem to have an easy life compared to their wild counterparts, but living in a human world comes with certain pressures. Teaching your dog basic skills and providing him with enough mental stimulation and physical exercise will prevent him from developing anxiety and other stress-related behaviors, such as destructive chewing, inappropriate barking, and aggression. But where do you even start when it comes to teaching, and how do you choose what techniques to use when there are so many different styles? The decision you make now will influence your puppy for the rest of his life.

There are three camps in the dog-training world:

1. Traditional training camp trainers often use equipment such as shock, choke, and prong collars to stop unwanted behaviors and teach new behaviors, as well as training methods that focus on intimidating dogs into obeying. They believe that dominance in dogs is a character trait and that behaviors such as pulling on the leash, going through an open door first, resource guarding, and so on is a dog's attempt to dominate the family and achieve the status of "top dog" in the household. They often call themselves pack leaders and encourage their clients to keep their dogs submissive to them so the dogs don't try to take over as leader of the pack. Traditional trainers focus more on punishing behavior that they don't want by using suppressive techniques, such as poking, kicking, hitting, shouting, yanking, and restraint, rather than finding out why the dog has behaved in a certain way and working with the dog to change that response.

2. Balanced training camp trainers use positive reinforcement in the form of food, praise, play, toys, and so on to reward and reinforce behaviors they like but will also use harsh punitive techniques to stop what they perceive to be negative behavior.

3. The positive training camp is where I pitch my tent. The main tenet of positive dog training is to teach our dogs what we want, reward what we like, and redirect what we don't without using punitive techniques or equipment that intimidate dogs or cause pain. We manage behaviors ahead of time and evaluate teaching

plans so that we can bridge the gap between what behaviors dogs want to do and what behaviors we want to see more of.

Positive training or teaching focuses on building a common language and teaching your puppy the life skills he needs to be successful in his environment. Puppies that have been dominated into complying with forceful training methods tend to be more insecure and emotionally disconnected. Trust is an important part of any successful relationship, but people are regularly given poor advice by traditional and balanced trainers and don't understand the damage that is done using punitive training methods.

Positive training doesn't mean you ignore your puppy's misbehaviors, but "discipline" should come in the form of constructive guidance rather than intimidation. Guiding your puppy into making the right choices and understanding what he needs to be happy will help increase the bond between you.

There seems to be a great misconception that positive trainers never like to say no to their dogs and allow them to get away with negative behavior. There is also a misguided belief that positive trainers only use food in training, which works with easy dogs but is ineffective when it comes to rehabilitating dogs with severe problem behaviors, such as aggression. If you've watched any of my shows or read other books I've written, you will know that this isn't the case. Positive teaching helps people foster relationships, even with problem dogs, by understanding why their dogs are misbehaving and using techniques that foster confidence by giving their dogs more opportunities. This changes behavior without damaging trust between dog and owner. Anyone can use rewards to teach dogs to learn, but it takes advanced knowledge and skill to turn negative behaviors around without the use of force.

People who make time to teach their puppies life skills lead more fulfilling lives with their canine companions. A healthy balance of learning manners, encouraging sociability, and providing your pup with the right kind of outlets will ensure his success. People who fail to give their pups the education they need are doing their puppies a great disservice and will have problems in the future. The learning process does not have to be costly or intense, and the more enjoyable it is for the both of you, the better the results will be.

UNDERSTANDING YOUR PUPPY'S BEHAVIOR

Behavior is "anything an organism does in response to a stimulus."[1] Every organism on the planet—from humans to wolves, dogs to insects, and plants to single-cell organisms—displays behavior. Whether your dog is jumping, barking, sleeping, eating, coughing, or performing tricks, it is all behavior. Your job is to help your puppy find behaviors that she enjoys doing, whether these behaviors are under her conscious control or not.

Take time to simply observe your puppy's behavior. What is your puppy doing right now? Is she looking at you, sleeping in her bed, or playing with a toy on the ground? Is she in your home or outside in your backyard? How is she responding to noises in her environment? Does she notice them or is she too busy investigating? Is she using her nose? Is her body tense or relaxed, and can you tell if she is happy or sad?

While people often associate dog training with actions such as sit, down, and come, these are really just specific behaviors that you can teach. If you attend a group class, you might hear the instructor mention that she will be "teaching various behaviors" throughout the class. What this really means is that she is going to help you teach your dog a specific behavior that you can ask your dog to perform, reinforce this performance, and then strengthen the likelihood that this behavior will occur again. This is sometimes referred to as obedience training, but I don't like using the term because "obedience" implies a heavier hand, and this is not the kind of methodology I use when training puppies and adult dogs.

I teach puppies and dogs basic behaviors to build up a language of communication, to strengthen the bond between puppies and their people, and to give the pup skills to function successfully in a human world. I don't want my dogs to "obey"; I want them to cooperate with me.

THE D WORD

There is a word that has caused many arguments and disagreements in the dog-training world. The word is "dominance," and the myths and misunderstandings about exactly what dominance in dogs is has caused many headaches for trainers like myself and had appalling consequences for dogs that have fallen prey to people's misunderstanding.

What exactly is dominance, and do dogs really want to take over our households and become higher than us in the "pecking" order? Is that why dogs guard resources, control access to space, and bite people when they are challenged? The answer lies in the fact that there is a fundamental flaw in the use of the term, because "dominance" is often used to describe a dog's personality—"Rex is a dominant dog" or "Stella is a very dominant female," even though dominance is a social "act" and not a character trait.

Dominance actually refers to a social relationship between animals of the same species and how a specific resource is allocated between these animals. It is only relevant when used relative to something else: "This animal is dominant over that animal in this situation."

Relative dominance in a group of animals can be extremely complex and fluid. Take two dogs in the same household, for example, and let's determine dominance based on which dog eats first and which dog has a favored sleeping area, such as the sofa. Often what matters to one dog—the food—is not as important to the other dog, who likes to sleep on the sofa. Dominance is all about who has priority access to what. That might mean priority access to food, a toy, bed, a person, or another dog. So the dog who values food most will want priority access and is the dominant dog when food is present. The other dog does not need primary access to the food and is happy to acquiesce in that situation. But around the sofa, the second dog is more dominant because he cares about where he sleeps and requires priority access to the sofa.

This is how relationships work in multidog households. Dominance and rank is dependent on who desires primary access to a valued resource, and dominance works to keep the peace because one dog naturally defers to the other in different situations, which avoids violence. In terms of evolution, violence in feral dogs or healthy multidog households compromises survival. If a member of the pack is injured because of a fight, this could affect the pack or group's ability to hunt and find food.

Problems arise between domestic and feral dogs when they both place similar value on a certain resource, such as a prospective mate or a bone. The domestic dog might accept regular eating and sleeping arrangements, but a bone is such high value that both dogs want primary access to it. Now we have a problem. This is why dogs in multidog households might be the best of friends most of the time, but fights will occasionally break out over resources. In this case the contested object or area needs to be taken away and managed so that the disagreement doesn't happen again.

Let's use a human analogy to illustrate what I mean. You have a director who runs a large and very successful company where his employees naturally defer to him because of his position. When he goes home, however, his wife rules the roost and his kids run rings around him. His status changes depending on the situation he is in. He is the dominant one at work, but his rank changes when he is at home. Dominance and rank is fluid and situationally dependent.

But how does dominance work between dogs and people? Are dogs really trying to dominate and achieve higher rank over us?

The answers to these questions are simple. Dogs don't view us as conspecifics (of the same species). They know this because we look, act, and smell very different to them. They are not deceived into thinking we are dogs when we do doglike things, any more than we are deceived into thinking they are humans when they sit on the couch or sleep in our beds. So why do we attribute so many human qualities to dogs, especially in terms of dominance?

Humans find it hard to just think from the dog's point of view and not impose their own feelings or ideas onto why their dogs behave in a certain way. We might say that dogs who growl, snap, or bite are trying to "one up" us or be pack leader, for example, and indeed some aggressive behavior does stem from the need to control, but if you put yourself into your dog's paws, you will gain a better understanding of why.

Dogs show these types of behaviors not because they want to "one up" you, but because they are either protecting something that is valuable to them and fear we will take it away or they want priority access to something that is important for their comfort, safety, and survival. Dogs bite for many different reasons, including fear, and the most damaging thing a person can do is to punish a dog that has bitten, or use pain and intimidation to show a dog who's boss and stop their perceived "ascent" to the top of the ranks. Punishment leads to insecurity. Insecure dogs are usually quite anxious, and anxiety exacerbates aggressive behavior.

Regardless of what traditional or balanced trainers say, all dogs can be taught with the same humane philosophy. The beauty of positive training is that it works on all kinds of dogs from Pomeranians to pit bulls and is especially effective for dogs that are anxious, insecure, and display aggressive behavior in the face of what they perceive as a threat.

Now that you know what dominance is, why should the correct use of the term "dominance" matter? Misusing the term shouldn't be that problematic. Unfortunately, there are so many myths and misconceptions that have arisen from the incorrect use of the word as well as acceptance of dominance theory that relationships between dogs and people have been damaged when people incorrectly assume their dog is trying to dominate them. This assumption leads to punishment techniques that people are told will be effective in lowering their dog's status in the pack. People think they are mimicking canine language, but in situations where one animal is dominant over another, the submissive animal voluntarily defers; there is very rarely any kind of violence among animals of the same species who have a social hierarchy. Violence happens in unhealthy relationships, and violent behavior breaks trust and damages the bond.

THE EMOTIONAL PUPPY

Emotions drive behavior, and behavior is our biological response to the environment and situation we live in. Years of scientific research have shown that dogs and humans have similar biological responses to emotional states, such as joy, fear, sadness, excitement, and pain.

Feelings are human interpretations of emotions, so even though we know that dogs have emotions, we can't exactly say how they feel. But because the physiological reactions to emotional states are the same as ours and because the physical expression of that emotion is also similar, it stands to reason that dogs also "feel."

Emotions stem from what is important to dogs and is a product of evolution. What resources does your dog desire and does she seek out what she wants or does she get frustrated when she can't have something she wants? How does she bond with other dogs and people and does she rely on you as her anchor to keep her safe and secure? Does she avoid things that scare her? How resilient is she in a stressful situation? How does she deal with pain and how sensitive is she to being handled? Does your dog jump up and down or bark loudly when she is excited? Does she prefer to be alone when she feels bad?

The physical expression of emotion is so similar to the way we express emotion that we can see when our dogs are feeling joyful and excited or when something is wrong. Pain is harder to recognize as dogs are good at covering their pain or have no way to tell us unless the signs are overt. Covering pain is an evolutionary trait and important for survival, as the weak often get left behind. If I work with a dog that is showing aggressive behavior, I will always ask for a full medical checkup first, including a complete blood panel, before I begin a modification plan. Too many dogs that exhibit nervous or aggressive traits are labeled as bad, dominant, or disobedient when in actual fact they are simply in pain.

Human emotions flow through a cerebral cortex (also known as the thinking brain) that is five times larger than a dog's, which might mean that a dog's emotions are a lot simpler than ours given that they aren't complicated by too much complex thought. This is sometimes compared to how a young child experiences emotion, leading researchers to state that dogs have the cognitive and emotional abilities of two- or three-year-old children.[2]

Your puppy's emotional resilience is strengthened by positive experiences. You shouldn't be overprotective but, at the same time, you need to be clear about how negative experiences at this young age can affect your puppy for the rest of her life. The brain doesn't erase fear memories. Even though negative experiences are specific to environment, people, or situations, dogs will generalize them to other places, people, or situations. For example, if your puppy had a negative experience because a man with a beard accidently stepped on her tail, she might become wary and fearful around any man with a beard, whether or not it was that particular man who stepped on her tail. Similarly, if a bee stings her when she's in the backyard, she might become fearful of being outside in any environment, not just your backyard. Negative associations will affect teaching success.

Fear is adaptive and helps keep your puppy safe, while phobias are maladaptive in that they serve no purpose and can actually damage her success. Cortisol is a stress-related hormone that is released during times of stress and is often only associated with a negative stress reaction, but cortisol can also be excreted during times of positive arousal, such as during play. Stress activates neural structures known as the sympathetic nervous system, making the heart beat faster and diverting energy-rich molecules to the brain and muscles used for fight or flight. If the puppy is in a relaxed state, her physiological processes are controlled by the parasympathetic nervous system. This is the state you want your puppy to maintain. Bouts of positive stress (eustress) that release cortisol into the body aren't harmful as long as the stress does not become negative and constant.

Puppies are likely to experience emotional changes as they grow, so providing them with a good learning foundation makes it easier for them to deal with any challenges they might encounter. Investing time at the beginning of a puppy's life allows that puppy to become a confident and well-adjusted adult and, while most pups cope well living in a human world, few people realize just how resilient their pet has to be to conform to the rules that domestic life imposes on them.

A LEARNING FOUNDATION

Give your puppy the best learning foundation by teaching him useful behaviors rather than focusing on suppressing or punishing undesirable behaviors. If your puppy runs up to visitors and nips at their pant legs, give your visitors a toy to give him as he runs toward them so that his focus goes onto the toy and not their legs. If your puppy barks at you for food, meet his need by finding ways to feed him more often or in more enriching ways so he doesn't feel the need to bark at you.

While you are teaching him basic learning skills, you can also use management to prevent unwanted behavior and set him up for success. Set up his environment so he can't practice an undesired behavior while you teach replacement behaviors, because whatever is practiced will become stronger. For example, if your puppy jumps up on people entering your home, put him behind a baby gate when guests arrive so they can come into your home without being jumped on. Focus on your puppy's strengths and enhance his natural abilities while encouraging him to learn behaviors that he needs in a human world. Teach him these behaviors at his own pace and in different situations, settings, and environments so that he becomes fluent and confident wherever he is. Be mindful of his body and vocal language, and keep the learning environment as stress free as you can.

Build your puppy's trust by teaching him that good things happen when he does certain things, even if you haven't asked him to do them. This will give him the confidence to behave in any environment and will motivate him to learn new things. Don't get into a hole by relying on punishment to teach him. This will only teach him to work as hard as necessary to avoid bad consequences. He might even try to get away from you as he associates you with unpleasant experiences, but he will exceed your expectations if he trusts you.

Good teaching starts with understanding what makes your puppy tick and using what your pup loves to build a strong relationship. At the end of the day, training is like a dance. When the two of you start learning the dance, you might tread on each other's toes, but when you know the steps, the dance flows beautifully. To get there takes practice, patience, trust, and a lot of work on both sides as well as understanding your partner and setting realistic goals and expectations right from the start.

CORRECTIONS

Should you correct your puppy's bad behavior? This is a subject that causes much argument among trainers, but in general, it's better for your pup's overall psychological health to instill boundaries without intimidating her or causing her to fear you. Remember that you decide whether a behavior is "bad" or not. Your puppy behaves in a way that makes perfect sense to her at the time, because behavior is a biological response to the environment and situation and is driven by emotions. It's your job to be less judgmental and try to understand why behavior occurs and what can be done to change it if it's something you don't want your puppy to be doing.

Everyone has a different idea of what is punishing, but an aversive is anything you or your dog finds unpleasant. What is aversive to one dog is not necessarily aversive to another, and what you might think is not unpleasant could be aversive to your dog. Some pups are sensitive to an angry look, while others find the removal of food unpleasant. Trainers who use shock collars to train puppies and dogs will tell their clients that shock collars don't cause pain and are not unkind, while other trainers like me will advise against them because of the body language we see in dogs that are shock collar trained and the wealth of research we have on the emotional fallout. We can argue among ourselves as much as we like about training methods and techniques, but a puppy doesn't lie and will usually tell you if she finds something unpleasant, even if this language is misunderstood or ignored.

So how do you stop unwanted behavior? You can offer a vocal interrupter or use the word "no" if you like. You can tell your puppy to stop doing something, exactly like you would a child. It's not the words you say, it's how you say it, and as long as you aren't intimidating when you are telling your puppy to stop doing something, she will respond without being fearful.

One of the most effective ways I teach pups and adult dogs to stop an unwanted behavior is to teach an alternative one. I will tackle that in more detail in chapter 5, but if a pup is doing something I don't like or in a situation that isn't safe, I will give her some alternatives and teach her what to do in that situation. It's a much more effective way of teaching, and it encourages learning new skills rather than punishing old ones.

THE POWER OF REWARDS

Regardless of what motivates your puppy or dog, rewards are very powerful in the learning process because they are part of a distinct and predictable motor pattern. Once your puppy eyes a reward, this causes a release of chemicals and natural opiates, such as the neurotransmitter dopamine, that makes your puppy feel really good. The anticipation of the reward creates drive. When your puppy receives the reward, he is at his optimum pleasure whether he is receiving a food reward or biting on a tug toy. That is why it can be hard for a pup to release a tug toy during play because the game feels so good.

I customize rewards depending on the dogs I work with. A reinforcer only becomes a reward if the dog finds it reinforcing and it increases the likelihood that a behavior will be repeated. I make a point of always marking behavior I like, and you can do the same with your puppy. I mark behavior with a vocal cue such as "yes" followed by a treat, toy, or game, or I just tell the puppy he did a really good job. This makes my pups feel good and motivates them to learn new things. If my dogs do something I don't like, I interrupt the behavior and redirect them onto something I want them to do instead. I then teach them how to behave more appropriately in a similar situation by giving them opportunities to learn new ways of behaving. This is far more powerful than punishing puppies for doing the wrong things. You expend far too much energy telling them off and miss an opportunity of teaching what you want your puppy to do instead.

Imagine if your schoolteacher only paid attention to you when you made a mistake. You may get A's most of the time, but a D grade is the only time you get your teacher's attention. This is just how people treat their puppies and dogs. They forget to mark good behavior and only give attention when the puppy is doing something they perceive as "bad."

The best way to eliminate a behavior you don't like is to use management. You can manage your puppy's environment and set him up for success so that he doesn't practice the behavior you don't like. Remember, puppies will do what works for them. Management dissuades your puppy from performing an undesired behavior while you figure out a teaching and behavior modification plan to change the way he behaves.

You can use food during the learning process, but over time other reinforcers can be used instead of food, including life rewards, such as going outdoors to play, playing with another dog or a human, or chewing on a toy. Most of all, I just talk to my dogs. They might understand what a few words mean, but the words I use don't really matter, because it's the way that I talk to my dogs that speaks volumes to them.

Communicating with Your Puppy

Speaking "pup" is all about making it easier for your puppy to understand you as well as taking the time to understand your pup. It begins by creating a bond through play, having fun, and making sure you and your puppy have good experiences together, while vocal and physical language can be used to bridge the human-canine divide.

The biggest mistake people make is assuming that their puppies understand them more than they actually do. Some dogs find understanding human language a lot harder than others. Humans communicate mostly through speech—we understand each other through words, which is effective if we need to communicate to a person that speaks the same language. But it can be noise to your puppy unless you have specifically taught her what a word or short phrase means or if she understands what you want just by the way you talk to her.

Imagine if your puppy tried to teach you about the world through smell. It would be virtually impossible for her to convey to you what she means through smell alone because our sniffing abilities are not as good as hers and we simply wouldn't understand. The resulting confusion would cause frustration for both sides and insecurity on ours. That's not to say that speech doesn't play an important role in communicating with our pups, because as I have said, we can teach them what certain words and phrases mean and the way we talk to them can be full of meaning.

I often talk to my dogs in my "mushy voice," especially when I'm greeting them after being away for a period of time or while I'm playing games with them. My voice will be light in tone, my pitch will be higher than normal, and my body language and facial expressions will complement what I'm saying. My dogs respond by wagging their tails, dipping their heads, wiggling their bodies, and spinning around so that I can pet them. Their mouths are usually open in a relaxed smile, and their eyes are bright and soft. They know that I love them just by the way I'm talking to them and the way I am moving too, but the tone of my speech sets the meaning.

Your personality can have a dramatic effect on your pup's behavior. Because dogs have adapted to read human signals, they are extremely sensitive to our attentional and emotional states. The more extroverted you are, the more attentive your puppy will be, but if you have a more introverted personality that inhibits your communicative abilities, your pup might struggle to understand you.

Some studies have shown that people who are less confident and less independent minded have dogs with more behavioral problems. People who are shy, anxious, tense, neurotic, or aggressive may also induce nervousness, anxiety, and aggression in their dogs. Neurotic or lazy owners tend to have dogs that are less responsive, while conscientious handlers have dogs that are easier to teach. Of course, these studies are looking at how people with different personalities respond to their dogs and vice versa, but environment also plays a large part. There might be a tendency for dogs to reflect or be affected by the personalities of their owners, but that depends on how sensitive each individual dog is to their owner's changing emotional states.[3]

Whatever your personality, be clear with the gestures and vocal cues you use with your puppy. Talk to her as much as you like when you are just having a conversation with her, because even though she might not understand what you are saying, she will certainly recognize the tone and pitch of your voice. However, when you are asking her to do something, use easy phrases or a simple cue word, which will make it easier for her to understand what you need her to do.

USING VOCAL CUES

"Sit! Sit! Sit!" Have you ever asked your pup to sit and when he doesn't respond, you repeat the cue again and again, getting louder and louder each time you say it? If you think he hasn't heard you or is being stubborn by not responding, you're not alone. "Sit! Sit! Sit!" seems to have become a very popular cue, but by repeating the word you are actually teaching your pup a delayed sit. Instead of your puppy sitting the first time you ask him to, the vocal cue has now become "sit, sit, sit." This is not usually a problem until you are in a situation that requires your pup to respond immediately.

Vocal and physical cues are the perfect way to build up a language of communication with your puppy, but a lot can get lost in translation and even simple cues and signals can be misinterpreted. Puppies can learn to associate certain easy words with an action or an object.

USING PHYSICAL CUES

Pups respond well to vocal cues, but you can also use your body to communicate very effectively. Active hand and body signals are cues that can be paired with actions and behaviors. Passive behavior, such as simply turning your back and ignoring your pup's unwanted behavior, can be more effective than shouting and yelling at her when she is doing something you don't like. But be aware that your pup may be trying to tell you something important, and ignoring her can be detrimental if your puppy is anxious. What might look like demanding, obnoxious behavior at first might actually be something very different.

Some gestures that mean one thing to a person can be interpreted in a completely different way by a puppy, especially if the person gesturing is a stranger. Hugging, bending over to greet, petting a pup on the head, sustaining eye contact, and kissing can all be threatening if your puppy does not enjoy close social contact. Greeting a new puppy by allowing her to come into your space, smelling your hand, and only petting her if she invites you to, will help her become a lot more comfortable in your presence.

DOES YOUR PUPPY WATCH YOU MORE THAN HE LISTENS?

Most dogs respond well to vocal and physical gestures, but which one is more effective? Do dogs respond better to visual cues versus the spoken word? A team of researchers from the University of Naples tried to answer that question by training thirteen dogs to retrieve three named objects using a vocal cue or with a pointing gesture.[4] It was important that the dogs responded equally well to a visual or vocal cue, and only nine out of the thirteen dogs were successfully trained to respond to both and went on to final testing.

Interestingly, the dogs responded equally well to both visual and verbal cues when those were used separately, but when the word and signal were used together, the dogs responded much more quickly. In the most important last contradictory test, however, seven out of nine dogs chose to follow the visual pointing cue.

This research is the latest in a series of studies that show similar results. Dogs respond well to both verbal and physical cues when used separately and together, but visual signals seem to be slightly more effective, so be aware of how your dog responds to your body language and think about what you are doing when you issue a verbal cue. Your dog might not be responding to the verbal cue at all, but is, in fact, being cued by a change in your body that happens each time you say that particular cue. I have always said dogs watch us more than they listen to us, and it would seem that this is certainly the case when we ask them to do something.

CUES AND PROBLEM SOLVING

If your puppy is having difficulty responding to your cues, try changing how you teach. Even though most puppies are good at following human communicative gestures, for example, your pup might not understand what your pointed finger means. However, if you say your dog's name, look at him, and then look toward where you are pointing, he is more likely to comprehend what you want him to do.

Even when your puppy knows his cues but doesn't respond, his lack of compliance is not disobedience, being stubborn, or stupidity. If a pup doesn't respond to a known phrase or cue, he might be too distracted, does not feel comfortable doing the behavior in a particular situation, or just doesn't know how. You might have taught your dog to "sit" in the home, for example, but this doesn't mean he will generalize that behavior to other environments. You need to teach him the same cue in as many different environments as you can so he becomes fluent in the cue and the response regardless of where he is.

Puppy Language

Puppies communicate through a host of different signals including visual, vocal, chemical, and tactile ones. These signals provide a constant flow of information—a language of ritualized behaviors that communicate intent, reflect emotional state, and resolve conflict. In fact, most puppies and adult dogs would rather have resolution than a fight, and much of this relies on being able to manipulate their own bodies to communicate their peaceful intentions.

Similar signals have different meanings in different situations. Specific parts of the puppy's body work together to tell the complete story. Observe your puppy's entire body and take into consideration her current physical environment. Observe and read specific body parts and interpret signals in context before you draw a conclusion as to what your puppy is trying to say.

Breed characteristics can of course complicate the message. Dogs' faces are not as expressive as ours because of their long or short muzzles, and they can be hard to read, especially if they have certain facial and body characteristics exaggerated by breeding. Breeds such as pugs, bulldogs, mastiffs, and Saint Bernards are especially hard to read as their features have been so manipulated. This makes it even more important to observe what is going on with the puppy's entire body so that we can capture the whole picture.

When a puppy wants to resolve conflict or communicate that she isn't a threat to another dog or a human, she will use a series of what is known as appeasement (or calming) signals. These include turning her head away, yawning, sniffing, raising a front paw, scratching, blinking, lip licking, showing her belly, dipping her head, and pulling her ears back as a submissive gesture. You might see a puppy do this around an older dog, and it seems to work as long as the other dog understands the language.

Fear and stress signals are used in times of uncertainty and true fear. Some of these signals are overt and easy to read, including tail tucking, freezing, shaking, lunging, snapping, and biting. But there is some physical language that is easy to misunderstand or miss. When puppies are fearful or stressed, they might lick their lips, yawn, or flip onto their backs and expose their bellies. They might urinate, defecate, practice avoidance, run away, or refuse to eat. In some cases, their fear might manifest in aggressive behavior, such as snarling or biting. If the puppy chooses to put distance between herself and a perceived threat, she will lean her weight forward and show more overt aggressive behavior. If she retreats or keeps her weight back, she might be more defensive and fearful. All body language needs to be assessed in context so the puppy's intention is not misunderstood.

If your puppy yawns when she's not tired, licks her lips when she's not hungry or has just eaten, averts her gaze while showing the whites of her eyes, turns her body away if someone tries to touch her, scratches or bites her paws or another part of her body, or shakes off even though her fur is dry, she might be stressed. These behaviors are not always associated with stress, but anytime you see these behaviors, look at the context and ask yourself if stress might be involved.

Decoding Vocal Language

Research shows that dogs vocalize far more often than wolves. The function of vocalization serves many purposes, including communicating inner emotional states, social signaling, identifying threats, and warding away dangers.[5]

BARKING

Barking is a natural behavior in dogs and probably one of the most important traits that humans selected for when domesticating them. Dogs were our first alarm systems—alerting us to predators or intruders that threatened livestock, homes, and crops. We have encouraged and harnessed this vocalization to help us locate hidden prey and to warn us of impending danger, but we also want to turn it off when we don't need it, and that comes with its challenges.

Vocally expressive dogs often find it very hard to stop barking, and why do they need to stop since the information they are giving us is very important? Dogs bark to get our attention, alert us to potential threat, and communicate their inner emotional state or wants and needs. They bark to convey displeasure and to elicit responses when they get excited or anxious, or simply because they're bored. Barking is a necessary behavior.

There is no doubt that too much barking is annoying, but your puppy's barks have much more meaning and contain more information than you might think. Fortunately, many studies have been done about canine vocalization, and now we have a better understanding of what our canine friends are trying to say. One of the most important discoveries is that dogs bark differently depending on the situation, and when we really listen, we are naturally quite attuned to the meaning.

In a study published in *Animal Behaviour*, Sophia Yin and Brenda McCowan compared the sound of dogs barking when someone rang a doorbell, when a dog was left alone, and when a dog was playing with another dog or a person. They reported that "the harsh, low-frequency, unmodulated barks were more commonly given in the disturbance situation, and the more tonal, higher-pitch, modulated barks were more commonly given in the isolation and play situations."[6]

You might be more attuned to the subtle nuances of what different barks mean than you realize. One study took a variety of people and played them the barks of dogs they didn't know. Interestingly, they were able to tell what the dogs were feeling just by listening to a recording of the barks. This must mean that canine vocal communication is pretty similar across the species, and evolution has helped us understand what dogs are saying.[7]

MANAGING PUPPY BARKING

If your puppy is barking excessively, ask yourself why and listen to him because he might be trying to tell you something important. Is he barking in response to a dog he hears in the neighborhood or at a guest coming into your home? Does he bark when he's left alone or when he wants something from you? Try to identify the reasons he is barking and then make a plan to address them.

Use management to create an environment where your puppy barks less or give him more enrichment if he's bored. (You can find more on enrichment on page 191.) If he's barking at you because he wants to go outside, teach him to come and nudge your hand instead to tell you he wants to go out. You can do this by praising him anytime he naturally touches his nose to your hand and, if the situation is right, taking him outside immediately after he does it. You can also offer him your hand and take him out when he goes to investigate it with his nose. You can add a simple word or phrase, such as "You want to go out?" to the action, so that he makes the connection between the action of the nose touch, the phrase, and being let outside.

If your puppy is alerting you that someone is walking toward the house, thank him for doing his job and take over from there. Jasmine is an alert barker, and I want her to tell me when someone is coming onto my property. It gives her an important job to do, but once she has alerted me, I need to take over. I taught her to alert me and then stop barking, by setting the scenario up with a friend and allowing Jasmine to tell me with a series of barks when my friend walked up the drive. I then told Jasmine, "Thank you" and gave her a food treat to tell her that I was taking over from there. It took a few repetitions and real-life scenarios for her to understand her job, but we now make a great team!

If your puppy consistently barks at people walking past your house, you can manage this by closing the curtains or blocking access to the window. You can teach your puppy a reliable recall so that you can call him away from the window. Finding a way to fulfill your puppy's need to bark, and managing his environment to lessen that need, is a good start to modification.

Sometimes the best solution for a behavior that you want to modify is to use the problem behavior itself. If your puppy is already barking, teach him to "speak" and then "quiet" on cue. Teaching behaviors with an "on" and "off" opposing system sometimes helps pups understand that the behavior is acceptable under certain circumstances. Here is how I teach it:

- I "catch" barking behavior when my puppy is doing it naturally, telling him to "speak" while he is barking.

- As soon as my puppy naturally stops barking, I say "quiet" and give him a treat.

- I won't encourage my puppy to bark again, but I will mark when my puppy barks naturally, with the cue word "speak," and when he naturally stops, with the cue word "quiet."

- After a few successful repetitions, I will start withholding the food reward for "quiet" a bit longer than normal and will keep increasing the time I withhold it from two to five seconds and then from five to ten seconds and so on until I deliver the treat. This encourages my puppy to be quiet for longer and longer periods and ensures that I'm not setting up a behavior chain where a puppy barks to get food rewards.

Now I can practice in other situations and at times when the puppy is barking, as long as I understand what he is trying to communicate to me. Puppies require enrichment and exercise, which greatly reduces the desire to bark, but if your puppy barks for a period of time when you leave the house, he might have a problem being separated from you. This is when you should call in a certified positive dog trainer to help with separation issues that might get worse in later life if not addressed.

Separation anxiety is a very common behavior in adult dogs and a very difficult one to treat, but it can be prevented by teaching your puppy to cope alone for short periods of time, gradually building up to an appropriate length. Your puppy might whine and bark if you leave him, but if you meet his needs rather than ignore him, your puppy will gain in confidence. Try leaving him with something to do like play with a puppy-appropriate chew toy. Try leaving him at times when he has had plenty of exercise and enrichment and is happy to take a nap. If you overwhelm him with attention when you first get him and then leave him alone for eight hours a day when you have to go back to work, he won't be able to cope. In fact, eight hours is too long to leave a young puppy without getting a dog sitter to take the pup out for potty breaks and to make sure he is enriched throughout the day.

GROWLING

Most dogs will growl at some point in their lives, whether it's to keep another dog away from a bone, while being touched, or during play. Unlike barks, which vary depending on the context, growls tend to be more similar. Research has shown that aggressive growls are longer than play growls and play growls have a shorter pause between growls, probably because play growls are just mock battle and don't need to be sustained as much as the real thing.[8]

It's not a pleasant feeling when a dog growls at you, but not all growls are meant to warn or threaten. Some dogs just grumble more than others, and they do this in a variety of contexts—during dog-to-dog play, human-to-dog play, or while they are being petted. If the growl is low and sustained and accompanied by a tense body, hard, staring eyes, and lifted lips exposing teeth, take the warning and back away. The dog means business.

What do you do if your puppy growls? Our natural instinct is to tell the puppy off, but that is often the worst thing you can do. Growling is important information. The puppy is telling you to back away from something and if you punish the growl, you are essentially telling your puppy not to warn you. In fact, I'm very thankful when puppies and dogs growl at me because they are communicating their need for me to do something. I would rather they growl and warn me to back off than go straight to a bite. If you punish the growl, you are teaching the puppy to do exactly that.

So what can you do instead if your puppy growls at you? First of all, heed the warning and back away from a growling pup. Then ask yourself why she is growling. Is it over a bone or other resource such as a toy? Is it because she doesn't like being touched? Once you know the why, you can then work on how you're going to change the behavior.

Start by managing your puppy's environment and take away any food or toys that cause her to resource guard. You can then introduce a toy that is of less value and play with your puppy, sharing the game and the toy. If she growls when you touch her or pick her up you should take her straight to the vet to find out if she's in pain or sensitive when being touched on a particular part of her body. Once you have ruled out a medical cause for the growling, you can be hands off for a while and introduce touching slowly. (For more on habituating to touch, see page 70.)

Dogs understand the universal language of growling. A study by the Family Dog Project showed that growls have meaning in the dog-to-dog world too. Dogs were placed in a room with a bone and as they approached the bone, the researchers played a recording of one of three types of growls. The dogs backed away from the bone when the "this is my bone" growl was played, but they generally ignored the stranger-danger growl and the play growl, demonstrating that dogs know what these different growls mean.[9]

Chewing Skills

Jasmine came into my family when she was six months old. Five pounds of sweetness entered our lives, and we were overjoyed. We weren't accustomed to having such a young dog in the house as Sadie was nine years old at the time, but she settled in remarkably well and quickly became the love of our lives. All was well until I noticed that the edges of my kitchen cabinets and chair legs were rough and uneven. Running my fingers over the bottom corners of the kitchen island I felt the shape of little teeth marks that had gouged into the wood. It was unmistakable—five pounds of puppy had redesigned my furniture overnight, and the damage was considerable.

There is nothing more frustrating than finding those telltale teeth marks on your favorite chair or returning to a chewed-up pillow or sofa, but chewing is just one of those doggy behaviors that makes absolute sense to a dog and fulfills an important need. Dogs don't see value in a designer shoe or an expensive chair— chewing just feels good and is a potent way to relieve boredom, anxiety, or stress.

Chewing and mouthing occur when puppies use their teeth to manipulate an object. Puppies can chew and mouth with varying intensities. These behaviors are often referred to as "biting" by some people, but chewing and mouthing is normal puppy behavior and is typical of puppies in the transitional stage of development. It's how a pup explores his world because, unlike infant humans, puppies don't possess opposable thumbs and have to use their noses and mouths to investigate the shape, texture, and smell of new things.

Puppies chew as part of the teething process, which is usually between four to thirty weeks of age. Chewing on any object helps soothe the gums around the teeth, encouraging baby teeth to fall out and adult teeth to grow. During this period, puppies will also chew as a way of exploring objects, and like human babies, everything tends to end up in their mouths. It is very important that puppies and young dogs are consistently supervised when running free around your home and in a safe, chew-resistant area when unsupervised. Make sure this "safe zone" is close to busier areas of the home so your puppy doesn't feel isolated. If you can't find an appropriate room, consider using a crate that you make into a safe, cozy den and use sparingly so it doesn't become a long-term place of confinement. You can also set your pup up for success by removing any items in your home that he might be tempted to chew, such as cables, shoes, or kids' toys.

Intense chewing usually subsides around six months of age, but many dogs continue into adulthood, particularly if they enjoy the activity. Rather than scolding your puppy for chewing, it is much better to redirect him onto an object you are happy for him to chew. Scolding your pup could encourage him to escape punishment by chewing when you are absent and doesn't address the reason why he is chewing. If you catch him in the act, simply redirect him onto a toy or object he can chew on and quietly praise him for chewing on that object.

Chewing on inappropriate objects is almost always rewarding, and it doesn't matter to the pup if it's your shoes, handbag, or the remote control. Many people find their puppy's chewing annoying, but they only notice it when it affects objects they care about or occurs with increased intensity.

If your puppy is chewing because he is bored, provide adequate mental and physical stimulation. If your puppy is chewing because he likes chewing, redirect to an appropriate item to chew, but if you think he is chewing because he is stressed, provide environmental relief and consult a dog trainer or behaviorist.

Puppies love to grab things and run away with them, and of course a game of chase is the most fun of all. But what do you do if your pup grabs something you don't want him to have? You can prevent the behavior from happening in the first place by teaching your puppy a reliable "take it" and "drop it." These useful skills can be used to get the toy back without physical force and will help you avoid getting into a fun game of chase or tug with the item. Grabbing things out of your puppy's mouth may also teach him to run away and hide, or swallow the item as quickly as possible before you can get to him. (See "Mine!" on page 186 to teach your puppy the "take it and drop it" game.) Provide appropriate chew toys for your puppy to enjoy, but make sure they are durable and able to withstand heavy chewing.

You can keep your pup occupied and out of mischief by giving him a hollow chew toy with food inside while he relaxes in his safe zone or crate. Pay attention to the types of chew toys your puppy likes and give him times during the day when he can engage in active chewing, which will keep his jaws strong and teeth clean. If you have a multidog household, encourage relaxation and avoid potential disagreements over valued chew toys by giving each pup and dog a separate chew location, which will make chew time a lot more enjoyable and stress free.

Exercise and enrichment are so valuable for every puppy and can help curb the desire to chew. A tired puppy is a happy puppy who has less energy to indulge in destructive behavior. Find appropriate outlets for your pup's energy. Physical exercise is important, but mental stimulation is crucial. Enrich his life by playing fun games and giving him puzzles and interactive toys to play with. Find a sport or activity you and your pup love to do to help release any pent-up stress or tension he might be feeling.

If the above suggestions are unsuccessful, the chewing might be related to a medical condition or be a symptom of a deeper anxiety issue. Destructive chewing usually occurs when a puppy or dog is left alone or becomes more pronounced when alone and is related to feelings of isolation, loneliness, and panic. This is sometimes referred to as separation anxiety or distress and needs the help of a certified positive trainer or vet behaviorist who will design a comprehensive behavior modification protocol that can be tailored to your dog's specific needs. If you suspect the chewing is related to a medical condition, take your pup to the veterinarian for a full checkup.

By following these easy steps and managing your home environment, destructive chewing can become a thing of the past, and your furniture, wallet, and most importantly your puppy will thank you for it. Management, supervision, and redirection are the keys when teaching appropriate chewing.

Nipping and Mouthing Skills

Nipping and mouthing are often seen when puppies are excited and want to play. It might be cute when your puppy is little, but little mouths turn into large, adult mouths and a behavior that was once "sweet" now becomes a real liability. While chewing may be the best solution to the chewing problem, teaching a new puppy that puppy teeth on human skin is never appropriate is important. The solution is usually management, reward, and redirection.

Begin by managing your pup's environment so she can't practice the behavior. This might mean that you retreat behind a barrier if play gets too rough. Set things up so that you can easily put a barrier between yourself and the puppy, but only use this as a last resort since it may frustrate or even excite your puppy even more. Psychologists' research on "time-outs" in human children shows that "time-outs are usually ineffective in accomplishing the goals of discipline: to change behavior and build skills. Parents may think that time-outs cause children to calm down and reflect on their behavior. But instead, time-outs frequently make children angrier and more dysregulated, leaving them even less able to control themselves."[10]

Mouthing is often reinforced by people who like to roughhouse with their puppies while playing, inadvertently encouraging the puppy to mouth them during the game. This is all very well, but if you have children or know that the puppy will be interacting with other kids or elderly people at some point, you might want to think about playing a different game. You can't encourage mouthing on you during rough play and then tell your puppy off when she mouths a child. Double standards and inconsistent rules don't work with dogs, so if you don't want your puppy to put her mouth on a child's clothes or skin, you should avoid encouraging the behavior during your interactions. I like to use flirt poles or teach my puppy a game of tug as a reward for refocusing her mouth and attention. These are fun, active games that allow your pup to play with and mouth a toy rather than you.

The solution to stopping puppy mouthing is to teach your puppy to do something else other than mouth. You can teach your puppy a "closed mouth" cue or teach her to lick on cue because a pup that licks can't bite. You can do this by praising your puppy anytime she licks you and putting a word or phrase to the action of licking. Once she has made the association between the action of licking and the phrase, you can use the cue if she is nipping and see if she changes to a lick. This can be a difficult one to teach, especially if your puppy is very excitable, but it can be very useful in reminding your puppy that her nipping hurts. You can also redirect her to an enticing toy.

Tug is a great way to teach puppies when it's appropriate to mouth and when to wait. By teaching a puppy when to grab the tug and when to drop the tug, you can teach her to think before she mouths. Tug is a great game to play, but it's best taught with some safety rules right from the start.

Even though your puppy might not know what to do with a tug toy at first, she is sure to put her mouth on it when you first give it to her. This is her way of investigating how it smells, tastes, and feels, but a tug toy doesn't really come alive until it moves! Here's how to start the game of tug:

- Get down to your pup's level and keep the tug toy low to the ground. This makes it more comfortable for your puppy to play with so that she doesn't have to look up or have the toy waved in front of her face as you bend over her. If you can't get onto the floor, try sitting on a chair so that you are closer to her level.

- Start moving the toy from side to side in short, erratic movements and observe what your puppy does. If your pup dives after the toy, she is definitely interested and driven by the movement, but if she looks away or shuts down, the game might be too vigorous for her. Try slowing it down a little and see what she does.

- Tug is all about engaging your pup's chase and prey drive, meaning that she will become more alert, active, and excited when the toy is presented to her. Give her lots of praise for jumping on the toy and if she grabs it in her mouth, praise her and start sharing the game with her, moving the toy from side to side.

- Don't worry about winning or losing the game. Some people might tell you that tug is a bad game to play because it makes dogs aggressive or that you should always make sure you win or your dog will start to dominate you. While it is true that some dogs get so excited playing tug that it seems to turn on their "crazy" brains, there are no winners or losers. Tug is such a great game because you and your puppy are playing a cooperative game with each other and sharing the same experience. If you drop the toy, chances are your pup will pick it up and bring it back to you to play more so that the game continues. If she decides to take the toy away, she might be saying that she wants the game to end and that is fine—don't tell her off and either wait for her to come back, entice her to come and play again with another toy, or stop the game.

- If your puppy drops the toy at any time, say the words "drop it" and immediately give it back to her. (For more about "drop it" cues, see page 186.) This is an important life skill that will teach your puppy to drop things on cue. It makes dropping things a positive experience for her, because when she drops the toy, she immediately gets it right back. Once she is regularly dropping the tug toy, you can use the cue for other things you want her to drop, especially if she has something in her mouth that you don't want her to have.

If nothing seems to stop your puppy's mouthing, take yourself out of the game and step away behind a barrier if needed. Exit the area promptly, stay outside for a minute or two, return, and give the puppy another chance. Repeat as necessary. It's helpful to come back into the space prepared with toys and treats so the puppy has something else to focus on when you reenter the area.

Toileting Skills

Teaching your puppy where and when to toilet works well when there is a combination of consistency, common sense, and positive training protocols. While toileting outside the home makes perfect sense to you, everywhere is a toilet to your puppy unless you teach him where to go.

There are a number of ways to toilet train a puppy successfully, and it depends on where you live. If you live in an urban environment with no yard, you might want to paper train your puppy until he is appropriately vaccinated. When it's safe for your puppy to be outside, you can start to transition him from toileting inside on the pads to outside on the street. If you have a yard or a safe outside area, you can use a combination of training pads and outside toileting, or you can skip pads altogether and take your puppy straight outside.

Housetraining is almost entirely about management. Your puppy should either be confined to a pen, crate, or behind a baby gate, and supervised at times when he has more freedom to roam. He will need to go out regularly, ideally every thirty minutes at first. Take him out into the yard or outside on a leash. If your puppy doesn't toilet within five minutes, go back inside for a minute and then go outside to try again.

If your puppy toilets outside, praise him, and then play or walk him for a little before you bring him back inside and allow up to twenty minutes of unconfined time indoors with active supervision throughout.

After indoor unconfined time, confine your puppy to his crate or safe area so that you set him up for success by preventing him from having accidents in your home.

Don't yell at your puppy if he does have an accident and never rub his nose in his feces or urine because your puppy may learn to toilet out of your sight rather than understanding that he was toileting in the wrong place. If you see your puppy toilet in the wrong place, interrupt him as gently as possible and take him outside to finish.

Housetraining is much easier when the entire family helps out. To improve the odds that housetraining will happen quickly, it's a good idea to create a chart showing each hour of the day and who is responsible for taking the puppy out at that time. The same chart can be used to record whether your puppy peed or pooped or if there was an accident.

If your puppy is still having occasional accidents, stricter management might be necessary.

These are the keys to successful housetraining:

- ❧ Manage your pup's environment so that he can't toilet where you don't want him to.

- ❧ Provide your puppy with many opportunities to go in the right place.

- ❧ Reinforce good choices (for example, toileting outside) with play, toys, and treats.

- ❧ Limit confinement in a crate or safe area to reasonable lengths of time.

- ❧ Provide pads in a confinement space if your puppy needs to be confined while you are at work. Hire a puppy sitter to be with him at the times you can't.

If you want to paper train your puppy first and transition him to toileting outside, here's how you do it:

- ❧ Create an area or "safe zone" where your puppy can be confined when unsupervised. This can be either a pen or a small puppy-proofed room with the pup's bed or crate, food, and water bowl.

- ❧ Line the entire area with training pads. At first your puppy will toilet on any pad that is on the ground.

- ❧ Make sure you remove soiled pads frequently.

- ❧ Reduce the number of pads in the safe zone by taking one pad away every few days, leaving a small area without a pad. Because your puppy has built up a habit of toileting on the pads, he should naturally gravitate to the area where pads are still covering the floor, leaving the area where there are no pads clean.

- Puppies don't usually like to toilet too near where they eat or sleep, so ensure that the pads that are removed first are the ones closest to the pup's bed and bowls.

- Over the next few weeks, gradually reduce the toileting area by removing each pad until there are one or two pads left. Ensure that the remaining pads are the furthest from the pup's bed and bowl and change them regularly.

- Use a "buzzword" that your puppy will associate with toileting and quietly say that word (for example, "go potty") to the puppy while he is in the act of toileting. When he has finished, gently praise him and/or give him a favorite treat or toy as a reward. Be consistent with this word, and he will start to associate it with the act of toileting so that the word can then be used to encourage your puppy to toilet.

- When it's time to transition from toileting on pads inside to going outside, take a partially soiled pad to an appropriate outside area and place it on the ground. This will encourage your puppy to toilet outside while still having the comforting feel of the pad underneath his paws.

- When your puppy is confident about going outside, remove the use of pads completely.

- If you want to create a permanent toileting area in your home, gradually ease the pen to this area if it's in a different place so that your puppy gets used to toileting in that area. As you give your puppy more freedom, encourage him to use the pad by leading him over to the pad at hourly intervals and then less regularly as he learns to hold himself for longer periods.

- Your puppy should now be at the stage where he is taking himself to his pad to toilet or holding himself until he can toilet outdoors. This choice is especially important for smaller puppies and dogs that might not be able to hold themselves for long periods.

Be especially vigilant and prepared for your puppy to eliminate immediately after meals, after training sessions, shortly after waking, after vigorous play, during or after a stressful event, or when he gets excited. Some dogs that are otherwise well housetrained might still experience the occasional accident, but others will toilet because they are nervous, excited, don't feel well, or are scent marking their space. Please remember that in your pup's world there are no toileting rules until you teach them. Elimination can happen anywhere that is safe and comfortable and whenever the need arises. It's up to you to teach your puppy that he can only toilet on pads or outside, understanding that it's not the best experience for him to toilet outdoors when it's raining or when the temperature is too hot or too cold.

Recall Skills (Coming When Called)

Teach your puppy a good recall before you even put on the leash. Start by building a strong bond with your pup, because the stronger the relationship and trust between you, the more responsive your puppy will be. While the rules of learning apply across the board with all dogs, every pup has her own unique learning style. Working with her strengths, understanding her weaknesses, and organizing a consistent teaching plan will foster success.

Recall is the first skill that all puppies should be taught, before teaching them to sit or lie down, because it's the most important safety skill to teach. Puppies should not be off leash in public places until they understand that they have to come back when called, regardless of what they are doing.

Recalling a puppy or dog away from something fun is extremely difficult. When a pup is playing, seeking, or chasing something, her body and brain are flooded with hormones such as adrenaline and cortisol as well as highly pleasurable and addictive neurotransmitters such as dopamine.

Dopamine is a neurotransmitter that plays a major role in reward-driven learning, by encouraging a dog's seeker system and helping regulate a dog's movement and emotional responses. Dopamine is released into the brains of dogs and humans when they are doing something that makes them feel good. Playing with other puppies, pulling on a tug toy, or seeking some hidden treasure in the ground becomes almost addictive, making it hard for your pup to resist the reinforcement and even harder to stop when told.

Studies show that the anticipation of reinforcement for both pups and people can be even more reinforcing than the reward itself and makes it much harder for focused learning to take place. It's why some puppies are so excitable at the end of the leash. Dopamine release makes it harder to concentrate, think clearly, and control impulses. A puppy that is having fun will find it harder to leave what she is doing and come back to you. How many times have you answered someone's request for you to do something with "just a minute" while you complete your task? Asking your excitable pup to come back when she is investigating something amazing and waiting for her to respond is her way of saying "just a minute." She has something very important to do first before she comes back to you.

So how do you teach the recall and what do you do when you call your puppy and she doesn't come back? Does she run toward another smell and keep playing? You can start with this simple rule—recall becomes a part of everyday life. It doesn't just take place when you are actively teaching your pup—it becomes a part of everything you do. It is as easy for the pup to respond as breathing.

Recall your puppy in a variety of situations every day, not just when you are actively teaching her. Recall her in the home, outside in the yard, and when you are in the park. This doesn't mean you spend hours doing recall exercises. Building a recall habit is important, but constant repetition will just bore your puppy and make her less likely to respond. It means that when your pup makes the decision to get up from her bed and walk over to you, praise her. When you are playing in the yard and she fetches something and brings it to you, praise her and play her favorite game. When she recalls in training, she gets a game of tug with her favorite toy or the tastiest treat. The recall becomes so natural and so reinforcing for your puppy, she comes back to you each time you ask her.

So your job is to make coming back to you the best thing your puppy can ever do, and you won't achieve this if you have a confrontational or punitive relationship with her. Don't fall into the trap of getting angry when your puppy doesn't come back when you call. Allow for failure because, through failure, you and your puppy will learn. When your pup comes back to you, praise her, even if she has previously ignored you. Coming back to you and being by your side is your pup's "safe" place. You are her anchor, and puppies will naturally gravitate toward something that feels safe. Your job is to provide that safety whenever she is with you as well as give her the confidence to go away from you in stressful situations and environments that are unknown.

If your puppy doesn't come back in a particular situation, ask yourself what you could have done to make it easier for her to be successful and then go back to basics and build up to that situation again. Set your puppy up for success by avoiding situations where she is forced to fail. If she is not ready to be off leash anywhere, do not take her off leash. Don't expect her to succeed if you teach her for five minutes, put her into a field of smells, and ask her to come back to you. Build up the recall cue slowly and have it rock solid in distraction-free environments and in different situations before taking it to environments and using it in situations where it is harder for your puppy to focus on you.

THE TOUCH CUE

The touch cue is a fun way to recall your puppy. A nose touch occurs when a puppy touches his nose to the handler's hand. Preferred touches are usually closed-mouth touches to the palm or sometimes two extended fingers for dogs with smaller noses. Pups can be in any position when performing a nose touch. In fact, nose touches are most applicable when the puppy is walking or running toward the hand.

A nose touch is a form of targeting, or teaching your dog to home in on or interact with an area or object. In this case, the target is your hand.

Targeting has so many purposes, including moving your dog about a space, orienting your dog to an object, refocusing your dog, and recall. The beauty of nose targeting is its simplicity—all dogs can do it and this behavior is easy for both dogs and humans to perform and understand.

Capturing a nose touch is a great way to help a puppy understand that offering behaviors gets rewards. It's quick and easy for puppies and dogs that are curious, but not every pup wants to touch your hand, so don't get frustrated if your puppy doesn't get it right away.

Here's how to teach the touch cue:

* Extend the palm of your hand out close to your puppy, but don't push it into his face. Wait for him to come over, investigate, and touch your hand with his nose.

* Once he touches your hand with his nose, mark the action with a "yes" and then reward him with a piece of food.

* Once he's performing the behavior reliably, add a cue while your puppy is in the act of touching.

* Repeat this until your pup is responding reliably, and then say the cue word as you present your hand.

❀ Begin adding distance so that your pup has to move to touch your hand. This will help move your pup around and get him to come to you when you call him.

❀ If your puppy doesn't readily offer a nose touch, use food to get him interested in your hand or the target.

Play Skills

There is nothing more rewarding than watching puppies play. Play is vital because it improves social skills, gives puppies boundaries, and improves coordination. Play is a bonding activity that provokes emotional responses that are incompatible with aggressive behavior, engaging a puppy's seeking system, which makes the puppy feel good. When puppies play with objects, their novelty, unpredictability, and complexity affect the amount and type of interactions with the object and may be related to any learning that takes place. When puppies play with people and other dogs, trust and valuable bonds are built.

SOCIAL PLAY WITH OTHER DOGS

Play fighting is like mock battle, where puppies change roles between "attacker" and "defender." The sparring might look quite rough sometimes and indeed, if your puppy is playing with another puppy or adult dog, you must supervise and watch for any signals that your puppy is uncomfortable or has had enough, but if both pups know the rules of the game, rough play is normal and healthy.

Marc Bekoff, professor emeritus of ecology and evolutionary biology at the University of Colorado, says that play in dogs is carefully negotiated and follows four general rules to prevent play from escalating into fights.[11] These are for pups to communicate clearly, mind their manners, admit when they are wrong, and be honest:

1. To communicate clearly, puppies signal to each other as they play. A play bow is how pups signal that they want to play and qualify that while taking a break in play, the behavior that is coming next is still play and not intended to do any harm. Reciprocity is an important part of healthy social play in dogs and if play is mutual, puppies will take turns rolling over, play biting, and chasing, and will share toys. There is a lot of trust in play between dogs, and that trust can be broken if both puppies don't communicate clearly.

2. Pups that understand the rules of the game will "self-handicap," as if to modify their strength so they don't overwhelm their playmate, inhibiting their behavior and keeping the "opponent" in the game. The objective is to keep the interaction going instead of stopping the game. When Sadie plays with Jasmine, Sadie will lie on her side and paw at Jasmine with her mouth open as Jasmine prances back and forth, launching mock attacks at Sadie's face and chest. Sadie is much larger than Jasmine, but Sadie knows this and puts her body into a position where she can still play but doesn't hurt Jasmine with her sheer size and strength.

3. Sometimes play gets out of hand, especially when puppies and dogs are young and don't understand the rules or don't have enough play experience. A healthy pup will "apologize" for accidentally hurting her play partner, and play will continue if the other dog "forgives" the pup for being too rough. Unfortunately, players that aren't socially confident can sometimes end up in a scrap if play language is misunderstood.

4. No one likes playing with a bully or likes being duped into playing, only to be hurt again or overwhelmed by rough play. Children who play rough quickly find themselves alone at the playground, and this is also true for dogs.

HUMAN AND DOG PLAY

Human-dog play follows the same social rules. People love to roughhouse with their puppies, and this is fine as long as your puppy isn't overwhelmed or gets so excited that he mouths at your hands and clothes. If you don't have boundaries for rough play, your pup will expect to play roughly with everyone and this might be a problem when he is interacting with a child or an elderly person. Even a gentle mouth on skin can be too much for a more vulnerable person, so it's best to start right at the beginning and find other ways to play with your puppy that doesn't reinforce mouthing. Directing play onto toys can help solve the issue. (See "Nipping and Mouthing Skills," page 101.)

Tug-of-war is a great game to redirect a puppy's mouthing (see page 103). Some people think that playing tug-of-war regularly with their puppies or dogs will make their dogs dominant and aggressive, but this rarely happens. One study showed that both tug and fetch scored higher on the researchers' "confidence interactivity" scale, which meant that the dogs were more playful, approached their owners quickly when called, and licked their owners frequently. Winning or losing the games had no effect on the dogs' scores.[12]

The study also suggests that dogs see tug-of-war as a cooperative rather than a competitive game, where human and dog work together to pull at or destroy a toy. Interestingly, the first study also found that dogs who engaged in more rough-and-tumble play with their owners experienced fewer separation-related behaviors.[13]

Social Skills

Positive socialization teaches important social skills, but overwhelming a puppy with too many social experiences too quickly may have the opposite effect and create a dog that hates being touched and fears interaction. Always be sensitive to your puppy's limitations, because sensitivity can make the difference between an adaptable dog that copes well in all situations and one that finds it hard to function in society.

Dogs are social animals, but this in turn brings its pressures because humans often have high expectations for them. We want our puppies to have good manners and be friendly with everyone, but people often don't understand how threatening and uncomfortable it is for some pups to have their space invaded and to be touched by a stranger. Puppies are very adaptable and most cope well with novelty, but some are less resilient, so be your pup's advocate and be sensitive to her experience. We want our puppies and adult dogs to be adaptable, confident, and emotionally stable at all times, but when they react negatively to what the person sees as "friendly" human interaction, they are often punished for displaying antisocial behavior.

Puppies are not born social animals, so they have to learn through early positive experience to bond with others. That is why it is so important to socialize your puppy well by allowing her to have great experiences with different kinds of people and other dogs while not overwhelming her. If you introduce your puppy to many things at one time, she might develop an aversion to being touched by people and other dogs. Good things must happen when people meet her for the first time, and introductions to other dogs must be done calmly.

SOCIALIZING WITH PEOPLE

It is very important that a puppy experience human touch from birth to promote a human-canine attachment and encourage the puppy's ability to develop social attachments with people as he grows. When a pup goes into a new home, every effort must then be made by the human caregiver to build on these experiences and gradually expose the puppy to new situations, people, animals, and environments. Human interaction also needs to be actively encouraged and supervised at this time so that the puppy has positive experiences with all kinds of people.

SOCIALIZING WITH DOGS AND ANIMALS

To optimize a puppy's social skills, good things must happen when your puppy meets other dogs for the first time. Puppy play groups and classes are a great way to teach pups important social skills and cues as long as the group is small and the puppies are matched in size and temperament, and not overwhelmed by the class bully. Some play groups and classes will not take puppies until their vaccinations are complete, while others start as young as eight weeks old—the prime period for socialization. Another option before vaccinations is finding a friend to have a puppy playdate with or take her on a trip allowing her to experience an outside environment in your arms until it is safe for her to walk in public. All interactions between playing pups must be monitored to guard against negative experiences, and all introductions to other pups and adult dogs should be made in a calm manner so as not to be overwhelming.

Building a solid social foundation is the greatest gift you can give your puppy and ensures that your pup is ready to tackle any challenges that might come her way, with confidence and a desire to investigate and discover, rather than to run away and hide. The more positive lessons learned at the beginning of a pup's life, the more resilient and adaptive that pup will be. Puppies are likely to experience emotional changes as they grow, so providing them with a good learning foundation makes it easier to deal with any challenges they might encounter. Investing time at the beginning of a puppy's life allows that puppy to become a confident and well-adjusted adult, and while most dogs cope well living in a human world, few people realize just how resilient their pet has to be in order to conform to the rules that domestic life imposes on them. Sadly, failure to follow these rules results in many adolescent and adult dogs ending up in shelters.

DOG PARKS

If you have a shy or fearful puppy or dog, the boisterous environment of a dog park may be too overwhelming. Well-meaning pet parents often believe that bringing their shy dogs into a busy, dog-friendly area will help "socialize" them, but the opposite is often true and a dog will become more fearful. If your puppy or dog doesn't do well in social situations, playdates with just one or two other puppies or dogs can be a much less stressful experience than a busy dog park.

Be warned! Even the best dog parks can be places where diseases are easily spread, so don't take your puppy to a dog park until he has had all his vaccinations. Once he is protected, don't take him to the park with all the big dogs. Unless he is a gregarious, large-breed puppy and can fend for himself, he is likely to be picked on and bullied by the adult dogs, so start off in a park that is just for small dogs. You still need to supervise him there to make sure the little ones don't take advantage of his young age and social inexperience.

If you have a pup that loves other puppies and dogs and is ready to hit the canine social scene, here are some tips to help you and your pup have the safest possible experience:

- Keep your puppy away from the entry and exit gates, as scuffles can break out when overexcited or overaroused dogs rush at newcomers.

- Keep your pup on the leash until you get into the off-leash area, but be prepared to release him as quickly as possible so he can greet others freely.

- Your pup might love playing with toys but avoid using any toy in enclosed spaces—particularly in dog parks. Fights can often break out when a dog becomes protective over a valued object.

- Avoid taking food into these areas as squabbles can happen between dogs who desire first access to a tasty morsel. It will also prevent you from giving treats to other dogs—which their owners will appreciate.

- While dog parks are great places to socialize with other pet parents, try not to let your conversations take your attention away. Disagreements can kick off very quickly between dogs, and there is nothing worse than a pet parent who doesn't actively supervise or intervene if their dog is misbehaving or playing too roughly.

- Dog parks are not a safe place for children to play in, so leave them at home or outside the park with adult supervision.

- Keep visits to the park short if it's very hot outside or try some indoor games and activities instead. This is especially true if you have a brachycephalic (short-nosed) breed like a pug or a bulldog, as they have a short upper respiratory tract and are not well suited to exercising in the heat. Monitor your pup's water intake while at the park.

Be your pup's advocate! If your puppy is showing aggressive behavior or seems fearful, uncomfortable, or agitated, head home before anything escalates and seek alternative environments for your pup to exercise in or different activities for him to do.

Walking Skills

Taking dogs for a walk is one of life's pleasures. My dogs get so excited when I get their leashes out, because a whole world of smells and discovery awaits them; but some dogs with fenced-in yards rarely leave the house, and this lack of novelty can lead to all kinds of problems. Imagine how monotonous your life would be if you never left your home. No wonder our neighborhoods are full of backyard barkers!

Walking improves a dog's mental and physical health and is a great bonding activity for pups and people. Varying the types of walks you take with your puppy will enrich her walking experience even more and will prevent future problem behaviors. Teaching your puppy various cues for these walks will add predictability and give her the confidence to explore.

When my dogs first get outside, they are all business. Toileting is taken care of quickly, which gives them time to catch up on all the neighborhood news left by other dogs, animals, or people in the neighborhood. I wish I could see the wafts of air my dogs smell—a rich tapestry of scent that guides their noses and bodies on sometimes erratic trails to the source. This is the "sniffy" part of the walk where my dogs get to explore and investigate the world around them. After this part of the walk is done, it's time for me to lead the walk, which is probably more forward movement than my nose-driven dogs would like, but it's time for more physical exercise. This is the way I "share" walks with my dogs, and sharing benefits all of us.

We know that exercise helps release endorphins and opioids in the brain, promoting an overall feeling of well-being. We benefit from walking as much as our dogs do because our senses are also stimulated as we take in new information around us.

Leash Skills

Because dogs are so eager to explore the world outside their living room windows and walking is the most stimulating part of their day, they might forget that they are attached to you. Their desire to investigate is impeded by an annoying piece of rope that's holding them back and slowing down the promise of discovery. Dogs don't pull on the leash because they want to be pack leader; they pull because they're excited to get to where they want to go. The desire to get ahead and discover the world around them is very strong and a leash impedes that discovery.

People don't make ideal walking partners for most dogs since a dog's natural and comfortable walking pace is much faster than a human's. Having to walk calmly by a person's side when the only thing a dog really wants to do is run off and investigate the environment requires a lot of self-control. You can experience what it's like to impede your gait when you walk next to a toddler or alongside an elderly person. If you have things to do and places to go, you might end up getting a little frustrated as well.

Instead of thinking how annoying your puppy's pulling is for you, consider how frustrating it must be for your pup to lose the ability to act naturally because he is "tied" to you. That being said, all puppies and adult dogs need to be taught how to walk on a leash without pain or discomfort so that a walk is safe and enjoyable for everyone. This starts with teaching your puppy how to walk well on the leash.

Pulling on leash is often successful for pups because people inadvertently reinforce the behavior by allowing their pups to get to where they want to go when they pull. But you can change this by changing the consequence for your puppy. Make sure your puppy is wearing a harness that is fitted correctly so that it's snug but doesn't constrict movement and can't come off. When your puppy pulls, immediately stop and stand completely still until the leash relaxes, either because your puppy takes a step back or turns around to give you focus. When the leash is nicely relaxed, proceed on your walk and repeat this when necessary.

If you find this technique too slow, you can try turning in another direction. When your puppy pulls, say "let's go" as you turn away from him and walk off in the other direction. As you turn, encourage him to turn with you so you don't pull him with the leash. Motivate him with your body and a fun, excited tone of voice and he will follow you. When he is following you, give him lots of praise, and when the leash is relaxed, turn back and continue on your way.

Don't forget to mark leash behavior you want. When your puppy gets to the position you want him to be, say, on the left-hand side of your body, mark that position with a verbal "yes" and praise him or give him a treat. He doesn't have to be in a perfect heel position as long as he is walking calmly by your side or even to the side slightly in front of you on a loose leash.

Once your puppy is listening to you more, you can become unpredictable. This means your puppy has to listen to you at all times because he never knows when you are going to turn or where you are going to go next. Instead of turning away from him you can turn toward him, making sure you don't step on him. Don't forget to praise him for getting it right, because the better you make him feel walking close to you, the more he will choose to do so.

CHAPTER 4

Empowering Your Puppy

Choice is essential for successful learning, and every organism needs to have some level of control over their environment. Choice allows a learner to feel safe and a teacher to earn the learner's trust. Lack of choice can lead to learned helplessness, while too much choice can make puppies and adult dogs less responsive to human guidance.

Excessive human control and guidance can lead to dependent learning and increases the likelihood of the development of fear issues. Allowing puppies and dogs to explore, discover, and make choices—along with human guidance when needed—encourages a good balance of independent and dependent learning that increases confidence.

The Power of Choice

I love cycling with my daughter. We find different bicycle trails to ride on so we can cycle without worrying about passing cars, but what makes biking with her even more enjoyable is that she has fought so hard to overcome a deep-rooted fear. Now you might think that riding a bike is no big deal—millions of kids do it—but my daughter found cycling frightening. She had fallen off her bike a couple of times when she was younger, but had always gotten back on with plenty of positive encouragement from us. She continued to cycle on easy tracks even though she had tears in her eyes and hated every minute, so keen was she to show us that she could conquer her fear. We pressed on, encouraging her with plenty of praise and rewarding her successes. After each ride she exclaimed with great relief that she felt she was getting better, but was clearly not enjoying herself. Then for her elementary school graduation present, we bought her a brand-new bike—it was much bigger than her last one but fit her better. It was the worst gift we could have given her.

The first time she rode her new bike she was visibly upset. We took the view that she would eventually get used to it and just needed time to acclimate, but it soon became evident that the transition was too much and the experience was miserable.

I love cycling and regularly rode to and from school in all kinds of weather, up two very steep hills. Cycling was as natural to me as walking, and I couldn't understand why my daughter didn't enjoy something that to me felt so free. It was not until we bought the new bike, however, that the penny finally dropped and I understood why it was so hard for her to make the transition.

When Alex was cycling, she felt completely out of control. She was frightened of falling off or crashing into something. Even though we pushed her gently, it was still too much for a child who not only was uncomfortable, but had no input in the cycling decisions we made, including where to go and how far. I can't explain why it took me so long to finally get it, but when I did, Alex made a complete turnaround. It was such a simple and successful solution. Give Alex some control and allow her to make all the decisions—where to go, how fast, and how long. Encourage her to take charge and lead wherever she felt comfortable. It worked like a charm. The first time I allowed her to set the pace and the route, we cycled happily for over an hour.

When I first started training dogs, I taught them everything I knew. I began teaching every cue I could, including how to sit, stay, come when called, touch, watch me, and lie down. Once they had mastered these techniques, I taught them more useful skills. I gave their owners as much information as I could and blew their minds with fascinating facts about their dogs. I encouraged them to go on lots of walks, participate in dog sports, and join dog-related clubs where their dogs could socialize. And if any of the dogs I taught were reactive or nervous, I made sure their owners had plenty of control while working on desensitization and counterconditioning techniques.

I saw a lot of success and was pleased with how well I was doing. It had taken a while to perfect my skills, but I was a good trainer and my clients were reaping the rewards. All was going smoothly until I met some real challenges—dogs that were so terrified of going outside that they couldn't even put one paw out the door. I used all the techniques I knew, but some of the truly fearful dogs shut down even more and I couldn't understand why. I was being gentle and kind, patient and respectful, so why weren't these dogs doing better? They were physically fit and had been given a clean bill of health, so I knew they weren't in pain or suffering from something I couldn't explain.

Then one day I just stopped and did nothing. I remembered what I taught my students to do when they were greeting shelter dogs for the first time—just be—put the food away and just be with them. Sit quietly, play a game, or just let them discover their environment without interference. Then build up slowly and teach them gradually—organically and without pressure. Do not overwhelm them and always be aware of what they are trying to tell you.

Why was I not doing this with my fearful canine clients? Why was I directing everything in their lives and not allowing them time or space to figure things out for themselves and just be? Like Alex, as soon as I gave these dogs some autonomy to make decisions, they changed overnight. Instead of making a reactive dog sit and stay while another dog walked by, for example, I played a game with them, or just allowed them to choose what they wanted to do in the presence of the other dog and where they wanted to go. I allowed them to make the decisions they needed to cope with different situations; praised their good choices and gently removed them if they became too overwhelmed.

CHOICE AND AUTONOMY

Think about all the choices you have made so far today. What time did you get up, what clothes did you put on, and what did you eat? Did you go to work or did you choose to stay at home and read this book? Now think about your puppy's day and how many choices she has made. Did she choose what to eat, where to sleep, and where she went on a walk?

A human adult makes approximately thirty-five thousand choices a day, while a child makes about three thousand.[1] The more choices we can make for ourselves, the more confident we are because we have the power to make our own decisions.

Research shows that confident children have more self-control and are more likely to be healthy in adulthood. Of course you can't give a child complete autonomy to make decisions, but you can give them a "sense" of it. Counseling psychologist Nicholas Jenner says, "It is important to note that we are talking here about giving our children a 'sense' of autonomy, not autonomy itself. . . . It is essential that parents give their children a chance to seek for this 'sense' and make it stronger than the feelings of shame and doubt. Then and only then, will children have the confidence to pursue and shape their own ideas and plans."[2]

I'm not suggesting you give your puppy complete autonomy, but giving puppies more choices from a young age allows them to grow into more confident adults. Why? Because feeling helpless and having no control over your destiny leads to insecurity and anxiety. Having a sense of autonomy is empowering.

CHOICE THEORY

Choice theory states that we are motivated by a never-ending quest to satisfy the following five basic needs that are woven into our genes. These are to love and belong, to be powerful, to be free, to have fun, and to survive.[3]

Even though we are influenced by rewards and punishment, Choice theory suggests that we always have some capacity to make choices and exercise control in our lives. It teaches that we are always motivated by what we want at that moment and emphasizes the importance of building and maintaining positive relationships with others to create a shared vision. People who are motivated to pursue common goals are more likely to work collaboratively.

But how does Choice theory relate to our dogs?

So much dog training relies on the reward-punishment model. We positively reinforce behavior we like by giving dogs something they really want—food, toys, praise, or play. But do we rely too much on that model, and should we be thinking of other ways to motivate our dogs?

PROBLEM SOLVERS

Students at Princeton University were split into two groups and given a problem. The first group was told that they were going to be timed to see how quickly they could solve the problem. The results would be recorded. The second group was offered financial incentives. If they were in the top 25 percent fastest, they'd get five dollars, and if they were the fastest, they'd get twenty dollars.

The results were interesting. Group 2 took three-and-a-half minutes longer than Group 1 to complete the task. This was surprising because it's generally accepted that if you want people to perform better, you reward them because rewards sharpen thinking and accelerate creativity.[4]

But numerous studies have demonstrated that rewards and incentives in the form of bonuses do exactly the opposite. Why? Because rewards can dull thinking and block creativity. External and contingent motivators work in some circumstances, but they often do harm. This is one of the most robust and ignored findings in social science.

Daniel Pink, author of numerous books on work, management, and behavioral science, explains these findings. "There is a mismatch between what science knows and what business does. Businesses are built entirely around extrinsic motivators—around carrots and sticks. These incentive rewards work really well for a set of mechanical tasks where there is a clear picture and a clear destination to go to. But rewards by their very nature can narrow our focus and concentrate the mind."[5]

So are we limiting our dogs' problem-solving skills and creativity by focusing too much on teaching them with rewards (and in some types of training, punishment)? You don't want to have too narrow a focus if you intend to be a good problem solver because this can restrict your problem-solving abilities.

When you teach your puppy, an answer that is completely obvious to you is not always obvious to the puppy. It's up to you to make it as clear as possible by understanding how your puppy learns and setting him up for success. Rewards or incentives can be good for teaching your pup mechanical skills but might hamper success when it comes to dealing with more complex behaviors, such as anxieties, fears, and phobias. Behavior issues are better served when teachers broaden their vision and think outside the box. We can put more emphasis on encouraging our puppies to problem solve. We can give them more choice in their daily lives as well as in teaching sessions so that they see a wider picture without being hampered by too much human intervention. Sometimes you don't need to interfere—you can give your puppy the freedom to "just be" instead.

AUTONOMY, MASTERY, AND PURPOSE

Pink states that too many organizations are making decisions based on outdated and unexamined assumptions that are not rooted in science. The solution is not to do more of the wrong things (like enticing employees with a sweeter carrot or poking them with a sharper stick), but to have new operation systems. The keys to intrinsic motivation—or the desire to do something because it matters—are autonomy, mastery, and purpose.[6]

These keys are the building blocks for a new system in business and a new way of looking at how we can motivate ourselves and our dogs. Autonomy is the urge to direct our own lives, mastery is the desire to get better and better at something that matters, and purpose is the yearning to do what we do in the service of something larger than ourselves. Traditional notions of management are great if you want compliance, but if you want engagement—self-direction works better. Half of Google's most successful products are made during "20 percent time," when employees are told they can spend 20 percent of their time working on anything they want. The freedom to create can have incredibly successful and lucrative results.

AUTONOMY FOR PUPPIES

How can we apply these building blocks to teaching our puppies and dogs? Positive reinforcement and rewards do work in many circumstances because reinforcement motivates dogs to learn, but too many rewards and too much human intervention can sometimes interfere with learning and destroy a puppy or a dog's creativity. When a dog is intrinsically motivated, they tend to be better problem solvers. Creative problem solvers are generally more confident, resilient, and emotionally balanced. If every aspect of your dog's life is controlled, she may lose the ability to think and therefore problem solve.

Think about what intrinsically motivates your puppy—what does she really care about? My Sadie is intrinsically motivated by her nose and loves sniffing her neighborhood. This is her favorite pastime, and she would choose it any day over food. Jasmine is intrinsically motivated by chasing squirrels and would chase every squirrel she saw if I let her.

HOW TO GIVE YOUR PUPPY CHOICE

Ask yourself the following questions:

- Do you micromanage your puppy?

- Do you think you hamper your puppy's learning by doing too much for him?

- Could you teach your puppy more successfully by focusing on his intrinsic rather than extrinsic motivators?

- Do you give your puppy enough choice in his life?

- Do you allow your pup to problem solve?

- Do you give your pup a sense of autonomy?

Your puppy will make many mistakes as he grows because mistakes are part of learning, but don't focus on these mistakes. Set your puppy up for success by redirecting him to something else and teaching replacement behaviors. Give him more choice in his daily life and discover what intrinsically motivates him.

You can give your puppy choices in training by doing the following:

- Let your pup direct the pace of a walk or let him take you where he wants to go, as long as it's safe.

- Allow your puppy to choose the game he wants to play by letting him pick which toy he wants to play with. You can do this by holding a different toy in each hand to see which one he's more interested in.

- ❧ Let your puppy end a training session with you if he wants to. If he moves away while you are teaching him, he might need a short break or want to stop altogether.

- ❧ Teach your pup to depress a button on the ground or ring a bell hanging on the door to tell you that he needs to go outside to toilet.

- ❧ Let your puppy choose where he wants to sleep and what food he prefers.

Even if you do just one of these things, you can empower your pup by giving him some control over his destiny, which will greatly increase his confidence.

CHOICE AND STRESS

Giving your puppy more choice also helps relieve stress. Stress is hardwired in all living beings, and we can't live without it. There is positive stress (eustress) and negative stress (distress). We build resilience in our puppies so they can cope with everyday stress and are more able to deal with the more stressful events they encounter. But too much stress can cause anxiety, shutdown, and distress. Chronic stress can truly impact a puppy's quality of life and lead to disease.

Positive training makes learning more fun, but depending on where and what you teach, you can still cause your puppy stress if you do or expect too much. If he disengages during training, you may need to look at where you are teaching him. Are there too many distractions in the environment for him to concentrate? Is the dog across the room staring at him and making him feel uncomfortable? Is the ground too slippery, or is his harness too tight? Does your puppy feel unwell and just can't tell you?

Please don't rush to judgment if your puppy refuses to do something. Look at your environment instead and observe your pup's body language to better understand what he is trying to tell you.

PROBLEM SOLVING FOR YOUR PUPPY

If your puppy's behavior concerns you, then you must find out why and get help from a certified positive dog trainer. They will give you ideas on how to manage your pup's environment so she feels more confident and doesn't rehearse negative behavior. A good trainer will help you discover your pup's intrinsic and extrinsic motivators and empower her with more choice in her daily life.

By setting your puppy up for success, you can focus on reinforcing her successes rather than correcting her mistakes. You can encourage learning by providing incentives when teaching your puppy mechanical skills as well as focusing on your puppy's intrinsic motivators to help her problem solve. For example, if your puppy is nose driven and loves to sniff, you can lay out a series of boxes and hide a treat or a toy in one of them. You can then release your puppy to find the treat or toy through investigation. Once she has located the correct box, you can redo the challenge, hiding the goods in a different box, and ask her to go search again. You might match the food or toy with a certain scent so that she begins to associate the scent with things she loves to play with or to eat. Once she becomes proficient at finding the food or toy with the scent, you can remove them altogether and reward her with either one when she alerts you that she has found the scent you asked her to find. This is the beginning of scent work and intrinsically motivates nose-driven dogs as well as rewarding them for their work. Giving your puppy more choice to explore environments with her nose allows her to be successful at doing something she loves, which leads to a greater sense of autonomy, confidence, and security. (You can find more problem-solving challenges in "Choice-Centered Training" on page 156.)

Intelligence and the Five Cognitive Dimensions

Cognition is how your dog's mind processes the world around her. Knowing your dog's cognitive style can help you understand how she perceives the world and what her capabilities are. Cognitive science is the study of mind and intelligence, embracing philosophy, psychology, artificial intelligence, neuroscience, linguistics, and anthropology.

CANINE INTELLIGENCE

An animal's intelligence is measured relative to the skills it needs to survive. For example, a dog needs very different survival skills than a pig does to negotiate the world successfully, just like a crow needs a different type of intelligence than a monkey does. Neither species is smarter than the other; their intelligence is based on how successfully they adapt to the environment around them.[7]

Dogs have remarkable dexterity and flexibility as well as senses that are in many ways immeasurably superior to ours. Cognitive science has compared the cognition of dogs to the cognitive abilities of two-year-old children, meaning that your dog can think, problem solve, understand simple gestures, and make inferences in a similar way to that of a very young child.

Your puppy can make inferences from a very early age, though not all puppies are capable of making the same inferences and not all learn the same things and in the same way. Puppies understand human gestures and can learn what human words mean as well as use physical and vocal language to communicate. They can solve problems, copy the actions of others, and recruit help from humans when they need it. Since most scientific studies on cognition have used adult dogs rather than puppies, I focus on the cognitive abilities of adult dogs, but puppies quickly gain a cognitive intelligence that sets them apart from any other domestic species.

THE FIVE COGNITIVE DIMENSIONS

Canine intelligence moves beyond simple learning and into what we call the five cognitive dimensions:[8]

1. Empathy is about reading and responding to the emotions of others.

2. Communication is using information from others to learn about the environment.

3. Memory is storing past experiences to make future choices.

4. Reasoning is inferring the solution to new problems.

5. Cunning is using information from others to avoid detection.

EMPATHY

Empathy is the ability to feel what someone else feels. We feel the pain and happiness of others, and this motivates cooperative behavior. While dogs might not exactly understand our human experience, they do show consolation behavior toward other dogs and people. They can learn to discriminate between our positive and negative facial expressions and are aware of our emotional states, even if they don't understand what we're going through.

Dogs also have the ability to catch the emotions of others. This is a form of emotional contagion I mentioned in chapter 1. When you are sitting on a train and the person opposite you yawns, chances are you're going to yawn yourself. Yawning is a form of emotional contagion, and studies have shown that dogs will sometimes "catch" human yawns but never the yawns from other dogs.[9]

COMMUNICATION

The human-canine relationship is further strengthened by a dog's ability to read human communicative gestures as well as its sensitivity to human emotions. Dogs seem to understand what a person pointing a finger at something means from an early age, something that is a lot harder (but not impossible) for other animal species to do. This is due to the fact that dogs have close relationships with us and have evolved to read our social and communicative gestures, which is important for their survival. It is a skill that is easily learned.[10]

When a person reads a human face, their eyes wander to the left and land on the right-hand side of the face. Dogs also have this left-gaze bias when they encounter human faces and might have acquired this skill because the right-hand side of a human face expresses emotional states better than the left. Studies at the University of Lincoln have shown that dogs have this left-gaze bias only when they look at a human face and not when looking at an object or the face of another dog.[11] This ability might have developed as a way for dogs to keep themselves safe by reading the emotions of humans.

Reading intentions forms the very foundation of human culture and communication. At nine months old, a baby begins to understand what some human gestures mean. By a year old, that baby begins to mimic and use these gestures to communicate with his parents. Take a simple gesture, such as a pointed finger. If you really think about the action of extending your arm and pointing your finger at something, it means absolutely nothing, except for the fact that humans have attached meaning to the gesture. For a dog, who does not speak our language, following where you point your finger is a cognitive skill that has come from thousands of years of evolving with us and is a skill understood by puppies as young as six weeks of age.

Human social skills develop at around nine months. Babies begin to pay attention to what others are looking at, touching what others touch, and understanding simple gestures, like pointing. Babies then begin to point things out to others. After nine months, babies begin to imitate the behavior of others, acquire first words, make social inferences, and develop more flexible problem-solving abilities.

Social inferences require an understanding of communication intention, which promotes flexibility and problem solving. Dogs can also evaluate cooperative partners just by watching them play, compete, or even share food with others. They can detect which individuals will be the best cooperative partners, and will tend to choose a person who gives food or plays tug over one who doesn't. When a family member complains that their dog pays more attention to another family member, I always ask how much time they spend playing, feeding, or interacting with their dog. If the reply is, "Not much," they have their answer.

MEMORY

There is no question that dogs remember several aspects of their daily lives, including walks they take, activities they engage in, objects they chew on, and treats they hide. Without short-term and long-term memories, those activities would be vastly impaired, and even basic things, like recognizing familiar smells and people or learning new things, would be impossible.

Olfactory Memory

Smell is closely linked to emotional memory. Think about a smell in your life that evokes a positive or negative feeling. The smell of rain falling on hot tarmac evokes memories of my childhood. I grew up next to the Wimbledon tennis complex, and tennis was our sport, particularly during the championship fortnight. It always rains at some point during Wimbledon, and if the day has been particularly hot and sunny, the rain produces a rich smell from the heated ground. This smells good to me and evokes the most wonderful childhood memories. Whenever I go to the dentist, however, the smell of the surgery reminds me of how terrified I used to be when it was time to get my teeth cleaned.

If smell evokes strong memories in people, surely it also evokes them in dogs. We know their sense of smell dominates their lives, so it stands to reason that their emotional experience of smell may be much more intense than we realize.

Auditory Memory

Auditory memory is especially useful when it comes to remembering the sound, tone, and pitch of a human vocal signal linked to a certain action or behavior. Once you have built an association with a spoken word and an action, you should continue to reinforce the auditory cue until your puppy completely understands the association. You can also communicate your intent and emotional state with the tone and pitch of your voice even if your pup doesn't understand the words you are using.

Working Memory

Working or short-term memory in humans has been found to correlate with skills in learning, math, reading, and language. Research has found evidence that in children, working memory is more predictive of academic success than IQ.[12] Studies of working memory in dogs is relatively new, but we know that dogs that can locate a thrown stick or navigate an area to find a hidden toy are more creative learners and better problem solvers. You can test your puppy's working memory by throwing a ball for her and encouraging her to go find it. If she remembers the general direction that the ball was thrown, she is using her working memory to find it.

Episodic Memory

Animals are believed to possess so-called episodic or autobiographical memories—a type of memory that serves to help us recall specific events of our personal history (for example, the day you got your first car). All this information is tied to specific places, times, and emotions and is bundled together so that you can reexperience the whole episode. These memories are saved without the knowledge that they have to be remembered in the future.[13]

Puppies and adult dogs need to memorize environmental landmarks so they can find their way around as well as construct mental maps of where these landmarks are located. Although dogs use visual markers to navigate their surroundings, they also rely heavily on how things smell. But visual mental mapping is important for remembering territory and territorial boundaries as well as for being able to navigate toward a food source or an area of comfort and safety.

Both my dogs remember things in their environment as well as experiences they have had long after they have happened. Jasmine likes to bury bones and toys in the backyard. These trophies can lay undisturbed for weeks before she returns to dig them up. Sadie remembers routes of walks we take as well as experiences that have happened along the way. She remembers where she was stung by a bee and becomes wary every time we approach the part of a hiking trail where she was stung, even when it's winter and there are no bugs. She knows the location of her favorite swimming hole even if we haven't been in the mountains for months.

Social Memory

Dogs need to be able to recognize other dogs, animals, and people. It's also important that they remember what various social cues mean, because the ability to read social cues allows dogs to function well in a social group. Dogs that don't have these skills often get into trouble because they can't read or respond appropriately to the social cues of others.

REASONING

Learning through trial and error doesn't take much understanding, but reasoning requires your dog to fully understand a problem and imagine a different solution. Dogs that are independent learners usually have natural problem-solving skills and don't rely on their owners to direct or help them. Dogs that are dependent learners tend to have better cooperative problem-solving skills and usually ask for help from other dogs or people. So what kind of puppy do you have?

Set up an easy challenge for your puppy and see if he solves it by himself or relies on you to help him. For example, you can put his food bowl behind a barrier so he can see and smell it but can't get to it. The only way he can eat the food is to find a way around the barrier. See how long it takes for your puppy to solve the problem. You can set your puppy any kind of challenge to find out what kind of learner he is. He might try to solve the problem by himself first and then ask you to help him if he gets stuck—a healthy mixture of independent and dependent learning—or the challenge might be too hard for him, and he will give up until you show him how to do it.

If your puppy finds learning difficult or is slow to pick up your cues, please don't think he's being stupid. Puppies and dogs do learn differently from each other, and your pup might learn in a different way from what is usually expected.

Modern-day dog training has certainly helped dogs adapt to living with humans, but it has at times created dogs that think less independently and rely more on humans to direct them or help them solve problems. If your pup is very independent and doesn't listen to you, you might need to play more bonding games, such as tug, or do more team activities together, such as agility training. If your puppy can't do anything without you, he might need more puzzles or tasks to solve without your help. In any case, a mixture of the two is good and can help facilitate learning.

CUNNING

The more cunning your dog is, the more likely she is to survive. This is because she has to solve environmental problems that might require a certain amount of deception. Many dogs are highly skilled at finding food, whether it's behind your back or while you are away. Large dogs are especially good counter surfers and are reinforced by finding yummy things on kitchen counters and tables. This behavior might be annoying for pet parents, but you have to admire a dog's ability. The cunning dog has good independent problem-solving skills and is often a natural hunter.

The Power of Sense

Your puppy's sensory experience will influence his behavior because each of his five senses is closely linked to his emotions. Emotions have a profound effect on behavior and can influence how your puppy sees and experiences the world as he grows.

I like to harness dogs' senses to help them learn and I call this process sensory education. This can be utilized for every dog, regardless of how proficient he is at using a particular sense. Sensory education can also help modify behavior and prevent behavior problems from happening. If you help your puppy accept and enjoy your touch as well as being touched by other people, he will have a better experience at the veterinarian's office or with the groomer. If he is uncomfortable in a certain situation or environment, you can change the way he feels by encouraging him to use his sense of smell to find food that you have hidden somewhere or placed on the ground.

To understand how you can use sensory education for your puppy, we must first take a journey into your puppy's sensory world. This starts with his most dominant sensory organ—the nose.

SMELL

Can you imagine living in a world dominated by scent? A dog's olfactory cortex is approximately forty times bigger than a human's, even though a dog's brain is just one-tenth the size of a human brain. Dogs have up to a billion scent receptors in their nose, dwarfing our comparatively meager six million.

THE SNIFF

Look closely at your puppy's nose and marvel at how her leather-like snout with wide, mobile nostrils (known as nares), gather scent around her. When your puppy smells something in the air or on the ground, she disrupts her normal breathing to gather scent, sniffing to retain more of the scent for identification. Her nose is cool to the touch, and scent molecules stick on the mucus that covers the outside and inside of her nose. These molecules dissolve in this mucus and are pushed up through the nose by tiny hairs called cilia. The nostrils lead to a bony, shelflike structure where the scent is trapped, and information is then gathered by receptor cells and sent to the olfactory bulbs and then on to the brain for processing. Expiration forces air out the side of the nares so that it doesn't disrupt the odors that are still on the ground.

ODOR LAYERING

Your puppy enters a room where you have been cooking meat and vegetable soup. He has already smelled it from the other side of the house, and the scent only gets stronger as he moves to the source of the odor. Once he is in the kitchen, he is assaulted with an array of different smells that your human nose has combined into one, but that he can separate into different ingredients. He smells the meat, the onions, the carrots, the potatoes, and the peas, and this incredible skill is called odor layering.

Alexandra Horowitz describes odor layering in her beautiful book, *Inside of a Dog: What Dogs See, Smell, and Know.* "It is not that smells are 'louder,'" she writes, "smells have different layers, which probably gives dogs a much bigger range of types of information. We might enjoy a painting from across the room but appreciate it in a different way when we can get up close and see the brush strokes."[14]

THE JACOBSON'S ORGAN

Dogs have a vomeronasal, or Jacobson's, organ located above the hard palate of the mouth just behind the incisors, at the base of the nasal cavity. Information received through this organ goes straight to the limbic system, which regulates mood and drives emotions and memory.

The Jacobson's organ detects pheromones in secretions located in the anogenital and other moist areas of the dog's body, including the face. These secretions provide information about the dog's sexual availability and are processed in the part of the brain associated with mating and emotions. This explains why dogs are so enthusiastic in getting to these areas when greeting. Pheromones also include information about a dog's age, health, and emotional state. Your pup might sniff these areas with her nose and then chatter her teeth, creating another opening for scent to enter.

There are some differences in how male and female dogs sniff each other. Male dogs tend to sniff the rump first because this area is vibrant with scent, while female dogs often go to the face first before moving toward the rump. Secretions from glands around the ears, mouth, and nose convey information that might be different from the information they can get from the non-bitey end.

Anal glands are located on either side of your puppy's anus and contain a strong-smelling fluid that is released every time a dog has a bowel movement. This secretion contains pheromones that give the sniffer vital information about the pup whose feces she is sniffing. When a pup is stressed or fearful, you might smell a slightly fishy smell from her rear end because she has expressed her anal glands. Sometimes these glands become impacted and need to be expressed manually by your veterinarian—hold your nose in the exam room when he squeezes the fluid out!

When either of my dogs urinate or defecate, they scrape the ground with their feet, releasing plumes of dirt and dust into the air (that sometimes gets into my face if I bend down too quickly to pick up the poop). Even if I can't see the dirt, particles are being disturbed as my dogs scratch at the ground, etching their scent deeper into the dirt as well as lifting the scent up into the air. All dogs have glands on their pads and between their toes. As they scratch, they leave their unique scent signature on the ground as well as in the air to cover a wider area. It's my dogs' way of saying, "We were here."

DOGS SMELLING HUMANS

Every person has a unique scent signature that is common to all parts of the body, and the majority of this signature comes from the fatty substance secreted by our sebaceous glands. Humans have sweat glands located in areas such as the underarms, genitals, back of the neck, and belly. These glands are activated by our emotional state, which makes it easy for dogs to smell how we are feeling. It's fascinating if not a little disconcerting that humans shed about thirty- to forty-thousand skin cells every minute, leaving behind a scent plume in our wake. Dogs can feel these wind currents as scent signatures billow around them.

When we are afraid of something, we produce chemicals such as adrenalin, cortocotrophins, ACTH, and thirty different hormones that cause the body to make changes to ready us for fight or flight. Our heart rate increases, blood sugar levels rise, and blood is diverted to muscles that are needed for action. The chemicals we produce provide a unique scent identification for dogs, enabling them to detect the human condition from a distance. Volatile chemicals dissipate more quickly in the air, but others remain and provide a trail for the dog to follow. This is why police dogs are so good at tracking people on the run. As the person is running, they leave many of these stress-related chemicals in their wake.

SCENT TRAINING

You can use your puppy's scenting abilities to encourage learning by playing scent games as well as doing scenting activities that will give him confidence and provide enrichment. The "go find it" game is one that can be played almost anywhere.

"Find it" games can be played in a variety of ways. You can teach your puppy to go find food that you've hidden in toys around the house. You can also encourage him to pick up food from the ground. These activities can be very useful in different situations. I use two different cues to separate the two games, but the action of seeking is the same.

GO FIND!

This is like hide-and-seek but with a toy or toys filled with food. You hide these toys in your house or backyard and send your puppy on a treasure hunt. Here's how you play:

- Fill an indestructible toy with delicious food and hide it inside the home or backyard.

- Make it easy for your puppy to succeed at first by letting her see where you hide it.

- When your puppy becomes more proficient, hide it in places that are harder to find.

- Challenge your pup to seek the toy out in places that are more difficult for her to find.

- Hide more than one toy around the house or in the backyard and encourage her to go find them.

Instead of always feeding your puppy from a bowl, you can put her food in a variety of feeding toys and hide them so she has to hunt for her dinner. This is a great way of giving your puppy physical and mental stimulation during mealtimes.

GO SEEK!

This is similar to "go find" but encourages your puppy to put his nose on the ground and seek out treats you have thrown down for him. This gives him a good activity to do in all kinds of different situations, especially if he's in a situation where he doesn't feel as confident. Doing something he knows in an unusual place will make him feel better. Here's how you play:

- Build up a positive association with the game by playing it during periods of calm, when your puppy is happy and relaxed.

- Throw a treat on the ground a few feet from where you are standing and ask him to "go seek." Once he has found and eaten the treat, throw another on the ground and repeat the exercise. Pups find it harder to see small pieces of food when they are thrown close to them, so most will use their noses to discover where the food is.

- Repeat the exercise at intervals, encouraging your puppy to seek out the treat. Don't do too much at this stage.

- When a positive association to the game has been built, you can use it in environments or situations that your pup finds uncomfortable.

- Only play the game when your puppy is calm and under his stress threshold.

- If your puppy gets too stressed and goes over his stress threshold, stop the game and remove him from the situation.

SCENT WORK

Scent work takes these games to a higher level. All puppies can do this activity, which not only builds your puppy's confidence and focus, but provides a safe way to keep her fit and healthy through mental and physical exercise.

Scent work starts with getting your pup excited about using her nose to seek out a favorite toy or treat reward hidden in one of several boxes. The treat or toy is then paired with a target scent—usually the scent of birch or anise. Once the pup makes an association with the target scent and food or a toy, you can just use the target scent alone. When your pup detects the target scent, the food or toy comes from you and not the box.

Once your puppy is good at the game, you can make it harder for her by expanding the game to entire rooms, exterior areas, and vehicles. As your puppy grows more confident with her nose, other target odors can be introduced.

WHY PUPS ROLL IN SMELLY STUFF

My family always knows when Jasmine has rolled in something. The normal after-walk ritual is pretty consistent. My dogs enter the back door and then turn around so I can take their harnesses off, but when Sadie is the only dog to come in and Jasmine is left outside, the family knows what's happened. Our normal ritual is disrupted as well by my quiet expletives as I prepare Jasmine's bath. Gloving up, I carry the stinking body into the bath and begin washing the stench of coyote poop or dead squirrel off Jasmine's body, replacing it with the scent of some delicious-smelling pet shampoo. This is the worst thing I can do for her, and Jasmine shows her disgust by rolling frenziedly in yard dirt as she dries off. How can I be so mean to remove the most delicious perfume from her body and replace it with an offensive, stinky pet shampoo?

Jasmine loves to roll in the smelliest stuff imaginable. As I realize with horror that her face and shoulder are beginning to sink into a pile of goo, followed by the rest of her body, I run as if in slow motion to stop her. But it's too late, and the stink of carcass now caresses her gorgeous fur and she is in canine rapture.

Jasmine is not alone, and rolling in poop or the carcass of a dead animal can start very early in life. Puppies do it, adult dogs do it, even senior dogs do it, and there are some theories that might explain this seemingly strange behavior. Dogs might roll in something that smells of the environment they are in to camouflage themselves and claim territory. Adopting the smell of another pack of dogs might make a dog more acceptable to the pack or make them more attractive to a mate.

Another theory that might explain why dogs roll in poop and decay is that it covers a dog's own predatory scent with that of its prey, making it difficult for the prey to smell the dog's scent, which, in turn, might make hunting easier for the dog.

I think Jasmine rolls in muck because it just feels so good. She seems to go into some kind of rapturous trance as she covers her body and then trots home like she's the dog everyone needs to take notice of. I think I'm onto something here because research has shown that rolling in smelly stuff seems to "spasm the neural circuitry responsible for play, sex, and eating all at once."[15] That's a whole lot of wonderful, which might explain why Jasmine takes any opportunity to do it, even though it drives me crazy.

VISION

How does your puppy see the world? The answer lies in the eye itself. Dogs have dichromatic vision, meaning that they can only see shades of yellow and blue. To process these colors, the brain responds to and interprets neurons in the dog's retina. Blue light shades detected within the retina cause suppression of those neurons, and yellow light shades cause excitement of the neurons. The brain responds to those signals with the colors we know as blue and yellow.

The cones and rods in the eye help dogs detect two colors. Human cones can detect the colors red, green, and blue. We don't know for sure how dogs experience the colors blue and yellow, but it's thought that they are more muted than the colors we see.[16]

Dog eyes have more rods than humans, which means they can see much better in low light. They also have a layer of eye tissue called the tapetum lucidum, which reflects light into the retina, meaning that the minimum threshold of light needed for a dog's vision is significantly lower than that needed for humans. This is important because prey becomes an easier target at peak activity times, such as dawn and dusk, so canine predators' vision needs to operate most efficiently during these periods of low light.

If you stand behind your dog, he might still be able to see you, depending on where his eyes are located on his head. Some dogs have a field of vision that is much wider than humans. We see about 180 degrees around us while dogs can see up to about 240 degrees.

WHAT'S ON TV?

A recent study revealed that over two-thirds of all American pet owners have left their TV or radio on for their pets. TV channels like DogTV have been specifically designed to be watched by canines. The colors and frequencies of the visual and audio content on these channels are specially designed to resonate positively with dogs. The content cycles through periods of calm, stimulation, and exposure. This ensures that throughout the time a dog is home with DogTV, there are periods of subtly increased motion and tempo. As a result, the dog will be periodically and almost imperceptibly stimulated, helping to minimize the boredom that can often result in destructive behavior.

This type of content is also interspersed with periods of "exposure" in which dogs might hear, for example, the distant sound of a vacuum cleaner played at very low levels, providing gradually increasing sound effects that effectively desensitize dogs to everyday domestic environmental sounds and help prevent noise sensitivities and phobias from occurring. TV for dogs can be company for dogs who are bored or suffering from separation distress. A dog's reaction to the content should always be monitored to begin with. If a dog barks at the content or rushes the television, DogTV is not right for them. Introduce the channel when a person the dog likes is present. This will help build a positive association between the content and the comfort that the person's presence provides.

TASTE

Taste and smell are closely linked, but taste starts with the tongue, and the number of taste buds varies drastically among species. Humans have approximately 9,000 taste buds, dogs have 1,700, and cats have 470. Many of a dog's taste buds are particularly attuned to meats, fats, and salts.

Dogs are essentially carnivores, but they will also eat fruit and vegetable material. There are many food temptations for dogs in our homes, and it's up to us to protect them and prevent them from eating food they shouldn't. Don't feed your puppy or dog any of the following: chocolate, avocados, onions, raisins, or grapes. These foods will make your dog very sick. Be very careful with artificial sweeteners too, such as xylitol, which is found in many foods, including candy and chewing gum. Xylitol can be fatal to dogs if ingested.

Dogs also have a sweet tooth and like the taste of chemicals in things like antifreeze and sweetened medications. Lock your medicines away, and don't let your puppy drink from puddles.

Meat has a very high salt content, so your puppy has special taste receptors for tasting water at the tip of her tongue. This encourages her to drink more but can also make her picky when it comes to what water she drinks and how she drinks it. Some dogs don't like drinking water from a bowl, especially if it has become stagnant, so make sure you give your pup fresh water every day. If your puppy still won't drink, she might prefer running water. There are many great fountain dog bowls that have a constant flow of water for pups to drink.

HEARING

Dogs are extremely sound sensitive, which makes them good at certain jobs but also susceptible to developing noise sensitivities and phobias. The human ear can detect pitches up to 20,000 hertz. Dogs can hear frequencies up to about 45,000 hertz. Dogs are born deaf, but puppies develop exceptional hearing and are able to pick up sounds from all directions within the first month of life.

Certain dogs are more sensitive to sound than others. When I was a child, I visited a farm every Easter and summer. I never wanted to travel anywhere else, because for me there was nothing better than helping the farmer work the sheepdogs. Max Jones had a large farm in the Welsh mountains and had thousands of sheep to care for, particularly during lambing season. His border collies, Roy and Sam, taught me so much about herding as well as how sound sensitive collies can be. They would range long distances from Max to gather the sheep, but they could still hear his whistles above the wind and driving rain of a Welsh spring day.

ACTIVE LISTENING VERSUS PASSIVE HEARING

Some puppies and dogs are unable to filter between active listening—the act of focusing one's hearing on a specific sound—and passive hearing, when there is a noise in the background that the brain hears but doesn't actively listen to. These pups can develop sound sensitivity or noise phobias.

As you are reading this, you may not be aware of noises around you, even though you are indeed passively hearing them. Now stop reading and concentrate on the sounds in your environment. Even though they've been there all the time, you haven't registered them until now because you haven't been actively listening to them. Start reading again, and after a while, your brain will shut out the sounds around you even though those sounds are still present. You may even be aware of them again, but they probably won't bother you if you're truly engaged in what you're reading. For a dog, the end result of this noise-desensitization process is that, even though she hears the sound of a thunderstorm, she is less bothered by it because it no longer overwhelms her. This sort of sensory education can be used when working with dogs that have already developed noise phobias.

SOUND THERAPY

Sound therapy is a form of sensory education and is a good addition to any behavior modification protocol dealing with anxiety or stress issues in dogs. Concert pianist Lisa Spector and Joshua Leeds, a noted sound researcher, have studied the effect of music and sound on the human and canine nervous system. Leeds states that "the auditory cognition in humans is complex but when exposed to music, the human brain methodically analyzes every interval, rhythmic nuance, instrumental density, and melodic turn."[17]

Innovative research has found that many of the same auditory cues also affect canines. Leeds and Spector discovered that dogs showed a preference for slow, simple classical music played on a solo piano at a low frequency. This music tends to discharge the nervous system, whereas loud rock music has the opposite effect.

TRADITIONAL SOUND THERAPY

Traditional sound therapy can be used for dogs that are scared of various sounds, such as the noise of a thunderstorm, fireworks, or loud city sounds. Thunderstorms are not easy to predict or control. A dog usually knows that a storm is coming long before a human does and becomes increasingly panicked as it approaches.

Condition your puppy to feel differently about storm noise by gradually exposing him to audio recordings of storm sounds at low volume levels and, if he appears relaxed, play his favorite game or feed him his favorite food. Allow your pup to play and relax in the presence of the soft noise for a period of ten minutes, take a five-minute break, and repeat the exercise. Introduce the audio at a low level again and, if your puppy remains relaxed and able to concentrate on playing the game or eating the food, slowly turn up the volume and allow him to become habituated to the noise without a fear response.

CANINE NOISE PHOBIA SERIES

The Canine Noise Phobia (CNP) series is a unique compilation of specialized audio recordings and innovative training protocols specifically designed to reduce and prevent noise phobias and anxiety in puppies and dogs.

CNP takes the process a step further than traditional sound therapy by pairing clinically demonstrated psychoacoustic calming music with gradually increasing levels of thunderstorm sound effects. This helps puppies and dogs acclimate to thunderstorm sounds in a controlled environment. The recording is uniquely constructed to enable dogs to "tune out" the sounds of a thunderstorm. In addition to treating already-present thunderstorm phobias, this tool can also be used to prevent thunderstorm noise phobia and other noise sensitivities from ever developing. The goal of this therapy is to change how a dog feels by altering the way she hears the sound. CNP encourages nervous puppies and adult dogs to passively hear the noise rather than actively listen to it.

TOUCH

Touch is the sense that facilitates bonding between dogs and between dogs and humans. You can convey different meanings in the way you touch your puppy. If you want your puppy to be more energetic, you might rub his fur quickly to get him excited, or if you want him to calm down, you can rub his chest slowly in a circular motion. When people are nervous, they tend to stroke their dogs in a fast repetitive motion, which is more of a displacement behavior to lessen their anxiety than it is pleasurable for the dog.

Puppies and adult dogs are very tolerant of being touched by all kinds of people, especially on top of the head, which is why I teach puppies to tolerate "rude" human greeting behavior (see page 72). We probably touch our dogs far too much, but social contact is important for building a bond and starts the moment a puppy is born.

A mother will lick and nuzzle her very young puppies to comfort them and stimulate them to eliminate waste. Puppies rely on their mother's touch for safety, to nurse, and to seek comfort in her warmth. When mom begins disconnecting, puppies will rely on the touch of their siblings to keep them safe. These reciprocated forms of touch are critical to the pup's survival at such a young age, and, as a result, puppies can become visibly distraught when separated from their mother or their siblings.

Some puppies are more sensitive to being touched than others. If your puppy flinches or moves away from your touch, he might be sensitive in that area or he might not like being touched. If puppies are not conditioned from a young age to accept touch, they may grow up to fear the touch of humans. You can tell if your puppy wants to be stroked by petting him and then stopping for a moment. If your puppy moves closer to you or nudges your hand, he is probably inviting you to continue. If he moves away or doesn't reach toward you, he is happy to be left alone at that time.

If you look at your puppy's face, you will see whiskers that are located above the eyebrows, on the muzzle, and below the jaw. These whiskers send sensory signals to the brain that give important information to your puppy about the world around her. The head and face is often a touch-sensitive area as well as the stomach and paws. Nail trimming can be a challenge, not because it hurts but maybe because dogs are as ticklish as humans when their paws are being handled.

Preventing Fear Behavior

As the modern dog's role continues to evolve from that of working dog to companion animal, there is more pressure on all dogs to cope and behave well in an increasingly busy human world. Dogs assume many roles in our lives, and it is up to us to make sure that they are comfortable in whatever roles they play.

Common signs of stress include lip licking, yawning, whining, excessive barking, destructive chewing, drooling, "dry" panting, restlessness, loss of appetite, sleep disturbance, nervousness, impulsiveness, reactivity, and aggressive behavior. If your puppy is overwhelmed by new places and unpredictable situations, or you are just looking for ways to encourage her confidence in different situations, the training and management solutions are very similar.

Set your puppy up for success by avoiding situations and environments that overwhelm her. Even the most confident pups can sometimes have difficulty during family celebrations or holiday events. If your puppy doesn't enjoy these social situations, create a safe zone for her, such as a gated-off room, which will help prevent stress and any behavioral problems that might be exacerbated by your pup's inability to cope. Think twice about taking her to places like county fairs, expos, dog shows, or holiday celebrations. While these events might be fun for you, it can be a very different experience for your puppy, and she will be much happier curled up on the couch or in her safe area at home while you go out and celebrate.

Most people would love their dogs to be social butterflies and not have to worry about who they bring into their homes, but a puppy that lacks social confidence still has to cope with novelty in the home every day. The delivery man, a visiting friend, children on a playdate, or a housecleaning service might make perfect sense to you, but strange people wandering around the home can be confusing and frightening for her. If you see that your puppy is stressed, make her feel safer by putting her in a safe zone or introduce her to new situations slowly, ensuring that she is kept under her stress threshold.

Start by having one friend over and allow her to interact in whatever way she feels comfortable inside the home and in your backyard. If your pup is nervous around people, take pressure off by instructing your guests to ignore her and stay out of her space until she makes the choice to interact with them. You can also arm your guests with your pup's favorite toys and food so she builds a positive association with their presence. Ask them to gently throw these treats or toys toward your puppy as they come in and instruct them to keep away from her unless she makes the decision to interact with them. If you have any reservations about how your pup might respond to new people in the home, keep everyone safe by putting her in her safe zone while your guests or home workers are there.

When you think it's appropriate, take your pup to a park or a less busy street and motivate her to discover the environment with things that make her feel good, such as your touch, praise, food, or toys. One of the best ways to do this is to encourage her seeking skills by playing games that utilize her sense of smell (like the "go seek!" game described on page 144). Remember to start in an area where your puppy feels confident. Use food if she is motivated by food and toys if she prefers toys.

One of the best ways to encourage confidence in different environments can come from watching what confident dogs do in these environments. If your puppy has a canine friend that she likes to interact with, take that friend with you on walks. Social walking is not only good for people, but there is strength in numbers. Merely following and watching what a more confident dog does in a particular situation can help your puppy's confidence. Small play groups give pups a chance to interact and play, but sometimes just a daily consistent walking schedule can help.

Puppies that are easily overwhelmed do best when things are predictable. Domesticated animals are amazingly adaptive, but every pup is different. While some might breeze through life being happy and confident, others find it hard to cope with new experiences. The more predictable the day can be, the safer your puppy will feel. Feeding and walking schedules are a good way to start as well as limiting visitors to only those your puppy feels comfortable with. Once she can cope better, schedules can be varied and new things or people can be introduced slowly.

One of the most important ways to help your overwhelmed pup cope better is to give her more autonomy and choice, which I explained in "The Power of Choice" at the beginning of this chapter. Dogs that are punitively trained have very little control over their lives, but even dogs that are taught in a humane way can find their lives completely micromanaged by their human caregivers, which makes them unable to make even the simplest of choices. But choice is valuable, especially for fearful dogs, and when they have a little control over what happens to them, they become more confident. Be a good observer and make a list of what your pup likes and what decisions she makes in different situations so you can plan for the future.

If your puppy practices avoidance, allow her to leave. If she chooses to go to her bed when you have guests around, give her the space to settle quietly and allow her some alone time. Think of all the ways you can give your fearful puppy choice and you will see a change in her, because choice is a potent confidence booster.

Be aware that confidence is not going to emerge overnight. Depending on how overwhelmed your pup is, she might never become a social butterfly or enjoy being in a crowded place, but positive social experiences can happen without the pressure of being touched by people or exposed to busy environments. If you are sensitive to your puppy's social barometer and her ability to adapt to novel situations, you won't put her under needless stress.

While it is important that your puppy be able to follow you around, which is a good habit to build for the recall cue, make sure there are times when your puppy can be separated from you in the house too. Independence training in the house also teaches your puppy to cope without you when you are away from home. Separation anxiety is not fun for dogs or people and is a very difficult condition to work with, so set your puppy up for success from the beginning by teaching her to be emotionally secure without you.

Choice-Centered Training

Choice-centered training is not a new concept, but it's one that I have used for many years to guide dogs into making better decisions in all kinds of situations. Because modern-day dog training is still polluted by the more traditional punishment-based methodology, choice-centered training has been somewhat pushed into the background, but the beauty of this method is that it works, and yes, even with aggressive or "red zone" dogs.

It saddens me how dogs are manipulated and pushed around. For example, I regularly see owners and trainers teaching their puppies and adult dogs to sit by pressing down on their backsides, or punishing them by poking, kicking, or restraining them on their sides or backs in an effort to dominate and gain control. The flawed idea that a dog will only learn to behave through force and fear is sad and misguided, but people are still misled into thinking that these methods are the right way to go. This leads to elevated stress levels that could be avoided if time was taken to understand how dogs learn and how they can be taught effectively. Choice-centered training is a beacon of hope in what is still a dominating world.

Choice-centered training involves catching actions and behaviors that you like and marking them with rewards that your puppy finds motivating. These actions and behaviors can then become the pup's "default" behaviors that he can use in certain situations. A default behavior gives the pup an alternative and makes him more positively confident in a situation that previously made him insecure. You can then expose your puppy to increasingly stressful situations and see what other behavior he offers. If the behavior is something that counters a previously undesirable behavior, the pup is rewarded. If he chooses negative behavior, he is quietly removed from the situation until he is in a place where he can learn again.

The only way Sadie knew how to deal with strange dogs when she first came to live with us was to lunge and aggress. Suppressing that behavior with punishment probably would have worked momentarily, but punitive suppression does not change the way a dog feels; it merely puts a bandage on the problem, which is likely to resurface again in a similar situation. Not only that, but it's simply wrong to punish a puppy or an adult dog for being nervous or insecure and only serves to make the insecurity worse. I changed Sadie's behavior by showing her that not only was there another way to behave, this way actually made her feel better.

I began by teaching her a variety of actions she could use, such as "sit," "walk on," and "watch me." I paired her success with rewards she loved, which ensured that her learning process was a fun and enjoyable one. I then taught her a combination of actions. Whenever she looked at a dog in the distance, I said "look" and rewarded her for looking but not reacting. I then asked her to watch me and when she turned her head toward me, she got another reward. After many repetitions (and a very kind friend who brought her dog along and worked with us), she was eagerly looking at the strange dog and back at me because the action was now reinforcing for her. I then phased out the food reward I gave her for looking at the dog and used it only at the end of the sequence—when she looked back at me. As the dog came closer, we continued with the sequence. At no time did Sadie have her back to the approaching dog. If Sadie reacted negatively at any point, I turned her away and took her to a place where she felt safer and learning could continue again. Because Sadie is highly motivated by food, she easily learned the process. We quickly got to the point where she could watch the other dog walk past with no reaction whatsoever.

I repeated the sequence with a number of different dogs, and when Sadie was ready to make her choice, I phased my cues out of the picture. Would she use the alternative behaviors I had taught her or revert back to lunging? I gave her a loose lead and stood still as a dog that Sadie had never seen before approached. Saying and doing nothing, I waited for her to make her choice. Each time she looked at the dog and back at me, I smiled and quietly praised her, but at no time did I issue a cue or do anything else. When the dog walked by, Sadie watched him and then looked back at me. I could see how happy she was and rewarded her for her bravery. She knew she had accomplished something that day, and as we continued over the next several weeks, her confidence increased and her new "choice" behavior became fixed.

I can't tell you how wonderful it is for me to see a dog learn, think for themselves, and grow in confidence through success. It's what makes my job so rewarding. Of course, I start the process by giving dogs alternatives, but at the end of the day, they are the ones that make the final choices. The beauty of this training is that it encourages dogs to think for themselves while gaining confidence from the choices they make, without being pushed, punished, or physically manipulated in any way. My presence was still important for many months, as it gave Sadie confidence, but she was gradually able to walk with other people and is now even greeting other dogs successfully on and off the leash. Lunging and barking was not only stressful for her, but exhausting. Her "choice," in comparison, requires little energy, and the rewards are much more satisfying for her. Sadie will never be a highly social dog because of her past experiences, but she now has a group of canine friends that has made her life infinitely more rewarding.

Choice-centered training is a great method for teaching all kinds of reactive and fearful dogs, but I also take pressure off by simply capturing actions or behaviors I like or using incentives to teach behaviors. For example, if I just happen to see a puppy sitting, I will praise her and reward her with something she likes. Nothing made her do it and it was her own desire to sit at that moment. This is called capturing a behavior. If I want to teach a puppy to sit on cue, all I do is find out what the puppy likes, be it a toy or a treat, and hold it in front of her nose. The puppy then has to work out how she is going to get the reward I have in my hand. She might try a variety of actions, such as pawing, licking, or nibbling at my hand, but she doesn't get the treat or toy until she puts her bottom on the ground. If the puppy is having difficulty understanding what she needs to do, I will move the food treat just a little above her nose. As she follows the food, her bottom should naturally touch the ground in the sit position. This process is called luring.

For so long, dog training has been about force, fear, and physical manipulation, which renders the dog into some kind of performing robot and doesn't allow the dog to think for herself. It might sound strange to those well versed in the more dominant style of training, but all dogs, regardless of breed and drive, have evolved to have excellent problem-solving skills and therefore have the ability to think for themselves, be guided to listen, take direction, and make the right choices.

As we learn more about what makes dogs tick, we are able to make their life experience better. Whenever I go into a home with a puppy or dog that is struggling to cope, I focus on finding ways to relieve some of the pressure she feels. Simple solutions, like placing the dog's bed in an area of low traffic or creating a "safe zone," can have huge benefits. Teaching families to tell guests and strangers to greet their dog appropriately gives that dog the freedom to make choices that make her feel good and promote confidence. Coaching children not to hug or tease a dog and allowing them to see what the world is like from their dog's point of view helps children understand and appreciate a dog's experience. Lowering expectations and understanding that their dog doesn't have to be sociable with everyone they meet helps the dog feel protected and secure.

What Would Your Puppy Say?

If you could ask your puppy how he felt about living with you and if he is happy with the amount of time you spend with him, what would he say? Would he tell you that you were the perfect companion or would he complain that you don't give him enough attention? We all lead very busy lives and our dogs have no choice but to fit into our schedules. This is fine for the dog that leads a full, enriching life with their family, but what about the ones who spend most of their days alone while their folks are at work? What would your puppy tell you if he could speak your language?

Dogs don't do well in social isolation. They are cooperative animals that do best in social groups where there is enriching interaction. Most dogs adapt well to changing social groups and situations, while others do not adapt to being alone. Even when you are at home, you might think you give your puppy everything he needs, but how can you tell if he's secure with the amount of time he spends with you and what behaviors do you need to look for that tell you that you need to do more?

Dogs are always communicating with us whether we recognize it or not. They do this by using vocal or physical language that directs us to what they want or are interested in. When your puppy looks at something, shifts his gaze to look at you, and then looks back at the object or place he was looking at, he is communicating his intentions through body language. Dogs will also help us understand what they want by using other physical gestures. Bowing down on their front legs with their behinds in the air often means that a dog is soliciting play from you or another dog, and if you respond in turn and start playing, your dog has successfully communicated his intention to you and you have responded appropriately.

If you find that your puppy is always coming up to you and demanding attention, often by just getting close and staring at you, leaning against your body, sitting on your feet as small dogs tend to do, or trying to climb all over you when you're sitting down, he might just need to be close to you at that time or he might need something more. Puppies can be demanding and will whine, bark, or get in your space to get your attention, but most pups just feel secure with the attention you provide.

Simply being able to touch you can make your puppy feel more secure. I call this need for closeness "anchoring," and it provides a security that makes dogs feel safe. Dogs will anchor themselves to other dogs, too, for safety and security. Jasmine will always sit or lie on Sadie when they are resting. The physical closeness makes her feel safe, and Sadie loves the massage she gets when Jasmine climbs onto her back. Anyone is fair game in our house. If you lie on the floor, you have to be prepared for a small dog to climb on top and lie down on you as if it was the most natural thing in the world.

If your puppy is not getting enough interaction while you are home or is being left alone for long periods of time, he might display certain behaviors. The lonely pup might bark, whine, chew, or tear up your home in your absence. He might start to get very stressed when he sees behavior that signals you are about to leave. People tend to be quite ritualistic when they are getting ready to depart and often do the same behaviors in sequence, like putting on a coat, picking up a bag, and picking up keys. These actions become triggers that signal your departure, so if your puppy starts to follow you around all the time and becomes restless before you depart, he might have issues with separation. Thanks to modern technology, it has now become a lot easier to see what your pup does while he is home alone. Webcams not only make it easier to see your dog, but some technology now allows you to talk to your dog while you are away and even dispense treats via an app on your smartphone. This might be all your puppy needs to help him cope, but if you still see behavior that worries you, contact a certified positive trainer that can help your pup with any separation issues he might have. With a little help, your puppy can live the happy and empowered life he deserves.

CHAPTER 5

The Ups and Downs of Adolescence

Your puppy is now moving into adolescence and, like any teenager, she is negotiating an awkward stage, and even though she is sexually mature, she has still not reached social maturity. This stage of life can be very challenging, and a puppy that once followed you everywhere and listened to your every word is now not coming back when you call, is marking inside your home, guarding her food, and starting fights with other dogs. It's no wonder that adolescent dogs end up in shelters as their families give up on trying to navigate tricky waters. But if you give your adolescent dog a chance, this is a wonderful opportunity to take her learning to the next level.

Adolescent Exuberance

A joyful dog is a wonderful thing to behold, but extreme excitement can be a nuisance for anyone on the receiving end. While training should be geared toward improving your dog's greeting behavior by teaching attention and impulse control skills, it should not dampen his joy and desire to socialize. Before you begin training, evaluate if your past behavior has contributed to the problem—a dog's negative behavior is often inadvertently reinforced by human attention. For example, if you allow your dog to jump and mouth while greeting you, it is an open invitation to jump on and mouth everyone else, so be consistent and employ a "no jumping" rule at all times.

Enhance your dog's attention on you by developing a repertoire of calmer behaviors to include in your everyday activities. Teaching induces a calming effect and will provide you with constructive tools to deal with his behavior. You can introduce everyday rewards, such as feeding or walk time, to enhance attention because focus must be given to you and impulse-control techniques employed before the reward is given. If your dog likes to chase balls, for example, give him the opportunity to chase a ball only after he has listened to your "wait" cue for a period of time. Waiting becomes a vital skill that will allow him to think and remember what he has to do before acting.

You can set up a ritual of behaviors on leash when greeting a person or dog, such as having him wait, approach the person when he is told to, and sit in front of them to say hello. If your dog gets too excited, calmly remove him to a distance where you can both regroup and try again. Keep repeating this exercise until he greets calmly, and he will be rewarded with the person's attention or by being allowed to go and play with another dog.

Adolescent Fear

I'm flying to Portland, Oregon, from Los Angeles and the pilot has just told us that there will be turbulence the closer we get to Portland. It is 53 degrees at our destination with rain and gusty winds. She tells us that our descent is likely to be very bumpy.

I used to be a nervous flyer, but the older I get, the better I have become. I virtually live on a plane because I fly all the time for work, but when I feel the first bit of turbulence, I begin to sweat. I can feel my heart beat faster, my stomach lurches, my breathing becomes shallow, and I don't feel hungry. I know that I'm experiencing a physiological reaction that is readying my body for danger. It's called fear.

I'm trying to keep myself calm as the plane makes its descent through thick clouds. I know the likelihood of the pilot losing control and the plane going down is very small, but my mind is now recalling every film and news story I have seen of planes crashing because of bad weather, and the fear begins to envelop me.

I'm also strapped into my seat. I know the safest thing to do is to remain seated with my seatbelt fastened tightly around my waist, but all I want to do is run away and hide and I can't do anything except sit here and pray that we land safely.

As I'm fighting against the rising tide of fear inside me, I think what it must be like to be a fearful dog that is restrained on a leash or confined in a kennel run. It is a powerless feeling. I have nowhere to go, no control over my situation, and no escape. The person who has control right now is the pilot, and I don't know what she's thinking. The only way I can get through this is to trust her skills, the plane's sturdiness, and the statistics that show thousands of planes experience turbulence every day and the chances of anything bad happening is very small.

As a human I can rationalize my fears because at least I understand the situation and have a vague sense of what is happening. It's going to get bumpy, but the chances are pretty good that I'm going to get to my destination alive and all will be well. It's believed that dogs don't have the ability to rationalize like we do and even though they don't watch the news or read books that foretell disaster and destruction and are unaware of what the danger might be, in so many situations, dogs have no idea what is happening and what is around the corner. We can't explain it to them. If they are fearful, all we can do is put a hand on them and tell them it's going to be okay, and if they trust us, we might be able to calm their fears a little. But it must be terrible to have so little control over much of what you do as well as limited choices to help you deal with an uncomfortable situation.

The primary function of the sympathetic nervous system is to stimulate a physiological reaction in response to a perceived threat. The sympathetic nervous system releases hormones within the body in response to stress, resulting in an "adrenaline rush." This "rush" activates the fight-or-flight response and increases blood flow to muscles, increases heart rate, dilates pupils, and gets the body ready to act. How we cope with this rush will either get us out of a situation or deeper into it, but if we're lucky, we make the right choice and we either practice avoidance or win the fight. If we make the wrong choice or have no control over the situation, we are in trouble.

But how do we combat fear in ourselves and in our dogs? The hippocampus is the central organ for learning (neurologically speaking). It lets in learning and adds new neurons by creating new connections between existing ones. The hippocampus is very sensitive to cortisol (also known as the stress hormone). Cortisol affects the rate at which neurons are added or subtracted in the hippocampus. High levels of cortisol, due to fear and stress, prevent new neural pathways from forming—thus preventing the learning of new behaviors. Put simply, when you are in a fearful state, learning cannot take place as effectively as when you are calm. Trying to teach or get the attention of a dog when she is fearful is counterproductive, but removing her from a scary situation and getting her to a physical and mental place where learning can occur again will help her cope. Encouraging her to seek, hunt, and problem solve will activate the learning part of her brain and quell her fear by discharging her nervous system and returning her to a calmer, parasympathetic state.

Many people still believe that comforting a fearful dog will reinforce the dog's fear, but ignoring dogs in their time of need can do great damage. We must be our dogs' protectors and extend a comforting arm to them as well as engage them in brain-enriching activities, which is exactly what I'm doing now. I'm writing faster as we are descending through the clouds. I know that if I activate my thinking brain, I can deactivate my emotional brain. Thinking, doing, and problem solving can quite literally turn off my fear.

I'm scribbling furiously as we descend, and it's helping. The plane is being tossed around like a boat on a choppy ocean, but with each bump and drop, I scribble faster because it helps quell my rising panic. I can hardly see what I'm writing, and the letters I am putting on the page are difficult to read, but at least this is preventing me from losing my mind. We are nearing the ground and the plane is being buffeted from side to side. The wings are vibrating wildly as we get close to the runway, and I have no idea if we're going to land safely. I'm praying to god, while keeping my head down and focusing on my writing as the wheels touch the tarmac.

We land.

Impulsivity

Dogs are immediate animals. If food is available, they will eat it; and if a rotting carcass is discovered, they will roll in it. Dogs will chase squirrels if they see them and will run out the front door if it's open. Self-control is not something dogs are born with, but lack of control can be fatal. The urge to run outside, chase something, or jump out of a car often overrides any sense of awareness a dog might have of his surroundings and can have devastating consequences.

Like children, dogs need to be taught self-control from an early age. They can easily learn simple boundaries and be taught basic manners in a humane and constructive way. Simply correcting dogs for "failing" does nothing to curb undesirable behavior and sets them up to fail again, while giving an alternative in the same situation stops unwanted behavior and allows them to succeed. Walking on a leash without pulling, greeting a person without jumping, or waiting while a door is being opened are all behaviors that are easy to teach with a bit of time and a lot of patience.

Impulsive dogs are easily frustrated and can switch attention very quickly. This leads to a decreased ability to sustain attention, leaving the dog more sensitive and responsive to distractions. Impulsivity has been linked to decreased levels of the neurotransmitters serotonin and dopamine, which affect behavior in a number of ways. Serotonin is formed from the amino acid tryptophan and is found in the dog's intestines, central nervous system, and brain. It controls sleep and awake cycles, pain perception, and mood. Dopamine is produced in several areas of the brain and plays an important role in motivation, coordination, sleep, mood, attention, cognition, and working memory. A lack of these important neurotransmitters makes it hard for dogs to focus and learn and increases impulsive behavior as well as restlessness, reactivity, and aggression.

The cerebral cortex or "thinking brain" is responsible for social inhibition and coping skills. The dog's ability to control his impulses and learn new things is compromised by his body getting "pumped up" with excitement or nervousness. Keeping your dog "under threshold" will help his self-control and ability to learn.

BEGGING

Impulsive individuals find it hard to tolerate a delay in reinforcement and will often react without thinking. This is particularly true around food. Dogs that grab at treats, dive into their food bowls, or beg at the table can be particularly difficult to control. When was the last time you enjoyed a meal at home without a pair of pleading eyes staring at you?

If you have a dog with a begging habit, it might be time to make some changes that can be accomplished with a few easy training techniques. The first thing to ask yourself is—are you part of the problem? Do you set a double standard by feeding your dog from the table and then expect her not to beg? As long as you continue to feed from the table or reinforce begging with food, however infrequently, your dog will keep begging.

So if you are ready to have a peaceful meal, you can start teaching your dog a new routine during mealtimes. Begin by creating an "invisible line" and set her up for success by teaching her without food on the table to start with and introducing it slowly.

This technique is also much easier if you have already taught your dog a "back up" cue. You can teach your dog to walk backward by doing the following:

* Stand in front of your dog with your legs slightly apart.

* Place a piece of food on the ground in between your legs and encourage your dog to move toward you and eat the food.

* Once your dog has eaten the food, she will naturally take a few steps back to look at you again and when she does, use a marker word such as "yes" and give her a piece of food from your hand.

* Repeat the sequence, marking and rewarding her for backing up.

* When your dog is fluent with the behavior at this stage, start using the cue "back up" as she is walking backward.

* After successful repetitions, you can delay the food reward from your hand until your dog backs up a bit further. Once she understands what the "back up" cue means, she's ready to learn how to stay behind the line.

Next, teach your dog to stay behind the line:

* Pick a spot away from the table and draw an invisible line that you don't want your dog to cross until you have finished eating.

* Lead your dog behind the invisible line, ask her to "stay" and then go back to the table and sit down.

* If your dog starts to walk toward the table, ask her to back up to beyond the invisible line again.

* At no point should you yell at your dog or physically move her in any way.

* Sit back down and pretend to eat while quietly praising her for staying behind the line. If she moves over the line again, gently block her with your body and encourage her to go behind the line again with the "back up" cue.

* When your dog is consistently staying behind the line, you can bring out some food and start eating. Try cold food first and gradually work up to the warm smelly stuff that is more tempting and harder for your dog to resist.

* Depending on how persistent your dog is, this technique may take time and numerous repetitions to get right, but if you are consistent, your dog will learn that she cannot cross the invisible line until mealtimes are over. You can make it easier for her to stay behind the line by giving her a food-stuffed toy or a chew to occupy her while you are eating.

* If you have more than one dog, teach this technique to each dog separately before putting them together.

So what happens if you have a dog that is just too tempted by the food on the table and finds it too hard to stay behind the line? Management is a great option. Put her in a crate, behind a baby gate, or in a different room with an interactive toy while you are eating.

If your dog continues to struggle with impulse control around food, or in any other situation, it might be because she needs other outlets to fill up her day, including more physical exercise or mental stimulation. Dogs will become ultrafocused on something because they have nothing else to occupy their time. Eating, jumping, door dashing, or stealing becomes highly reinforcing because those are the only activities that break up the monotony of the day. For dogs that are always hungry, the anticipation and consumption of food is what drives them. These dogs might benefit from having three meals a day instead of two or to have their meals fed via activity toys that challenge them rather than having food provided directly from a bowl.

Depending on your dog's physical health, you should consider adding an extra walk or game to her daily routine or even look into participating in a dog sport. Burning excess energy helps relieve stress and focus the mind, but always be aware that the more energy your dog uses, the more food she will need to sustain her.

Impulsive dogs often end up in shelters, particularly if they exhibit reactive or aggressive behavior. Having a short fuse or not thinking before reacting often gets these dogs into trouble. The key to success with impulsive dogs is to get them thinking or doing a task they find easy to focus on. If you think your dog is having difficulty learning and finds it hard to focus, it might be time to take her to your vet, who can rule out any medical cause for your dog's behavior; and then enroll your dog in some classes with a certified positive trainer.

JUMPING

Your guests' arrival is imminent and there's no time to put your dog away. The bell rings, your dog goes wild, and as soon as your guests come through the door, they're flattened against the wall by an exuberant greeting from a highly excitable and energetic bundle of fur.

Having been on the receiving end of many canine jumpers, I know what it's like. I've been pushed over, bruised, slobbered on, and nearly had my arm broken by an eighty-pound bulldog who jumped up on me as I came through the door, grabbed my wrist, and led me hastily to his dog bed. "Don't worry," his mom said, "he does that to everyone he likes!" I'm pretty sure she meant it as a compliment, but I was in too much pain to feel very flattered.

I love dogs that say hello with energy, and it's always a relief as a trainer to be greeted by a dog that's pleased to see me, but not all dogs that jump are eager for attention or social contact—sometimes jumping behavior can be a dog's way of coping with a change in the environment that makes her nervous. It's pretty easy to recognize an uncomfortable jumper, especially if you know how your dog reacts to new people. A nervous jumper exhibits much stiffer body language than a dog that is excited to see you and may eye guests warily as they enter his space.

Puppies are often encouraged to jump because they don't do much damage when they're small, but adolescent and adult dogs can really harm someone by jumping on them, so teaching your pup not to jump up is an important skill. If you have a jumping dog, there are ways to encourage him to keep four on the floor. First of all, you can manage the behavior by putting him behind a baby gate when guests come over. This is especially important for dogs that are nervous or if a small child or elderly person is visiting and you can't risk it. In other circumstances, you can teach your dog to greet appropriately by doing the following:

❧ Teach your dog to keep four on the floor at all times with every person he greets, including you. Sometimes pet parents reinforce jumping behavior by allowing their dogs to jump on them but telling them off when they jump on other people. There needs to be one rule for all.

❧ Give your dog something else to do, especially during times when he is most likely to jump, such as when people come to the door. The energy and adrenaline that drives jumping behavior has to find another outlet, so teach your dog a different activity when people first arrive, such as going to fetch a toy or running to a mat or bed and staying there until cued to come off. This requires a certain amount of impulse control and can be difficult for excitable dogs, but if you make learning fun and reinforce success with motivating rewards, you will get the behavior you desire.

❧ Teaching your dog cues to find alternate behaviors is key. A sitting dog cannot jump, so utilize family members, friends, and neighbors to help you practice sitting on greeting. Line up your volunteers and approach each one with your dog on leash. If your dog jumps, simply turn in the other direction, walk away a few steps, turn around, and approach again. If he walks up to a person and sits, give attention and a secondary reward, such as food or a toy, for complying.

❧ Start by teaching these basics in a quiet environment and with calm volunteers before taking it to where the jumping behavior usually happens, which in most cases is by the front door.

❧ Once your dog is sitting consistently as a person walks through the door, introduce auditory triggers that get your dog excited, such as a knock or bell ring. Wait for your dog to calm before opening the door and letting someone in to greet. If he jumps up, your "guest" will turn around and leave and the secondary reward goes away. If he sits, he gets attention and a reward. Only practice off leash when your dog is consistently performing what you need him to do and always expect failures—they're a normal part of the learning process.

If your dog is wary of strangers, keep everyone safe and comfortable by keeping him behind a baby gate or in his "safe zone" until your guests are settled. If he is wary but social, allow him to greet calmly, but if he prefers his own space, give him an activity toy and leave him in his safe area.

Don't knee your dog in the chest, yank her collar, shout, shock, or physically reprimand her for jumping. Even though these actions might "fix" things for that moment, they don't actually teach a dog anything and you will usually find your dog continues to jump when a similar situation arises. Teaching her what to do instead will encourage her to make better choices the next time she feels the need to jump up.

Reactivity

All animals react differently to different things. We give our puppies and dogs the life skills they need to behave appropriately in different situations, but sometimes dogs show an intensity in their reaction that is difficult to handle. It can be challenging to live with a dog that lunges toward other dogs or barks at people passing by. Even if we know why these behaviors happen, it's still frustrating and potentially dangerous when they do.

What exactly is reactivity, and why do we start to see these behaviors in adolescent dogs? Hormones and maturing bodies certainly play a large part, but young dogs can also react negatively to things they perceive as threatening, even if the stimulus doesn't seem threatening to us. Veterinarian Karen Overall explains that "reactive dogs respond to normal stimuli with a higher-than-normal level of intensity. The behaviors [used] to ascertain reactivity (or arousal) are alertness, restlessness, vocalization, systemic effects, displacement behaviors, and changes in solicitous behaviors."[1]

Dogs that are fearful tend to need more thinking time when it comes to evaluating a situation. This is the time when we say they are "under threshold," that their stress hasn't built up to the point where they go "over threshold" and react. Dogs are visual thinkers, and nervous dogs prefer to approach a social situation voluntarily rather than being pressured to interact. If the pressure gets to be too much or the dog isn't interested in social interaction, the dog will react.

Has your adolescent dog becomes restless in certain situations? Does she bark, whine, urinate, defecate, or vocalize inappropriately? Does she excessively lick herself, spin in circles, or chase her tail? Does she jump up at you or other people, lunge toward other dogs on the leash, or run up and down the perimeter of your fence? If you answer yes to any of these behaviors, your dog might be overreacting to things that shouldn't warrant such an intense reaction, at least from our point of view. We might consider the intensity abnormal, but it makes perfect sense to your dog.

"Reactivity" has become a popular term to describe these kinds of intense behaviors, but other terms are also used to describe dogs that overreact. People call their dogs "frustrated greeters" and "leash reactive," or say they're suffering from "barrier frustration" if their dogs bark behind a fence or inside a kennel run.

WHY SOME DOGS OVERREACT

Dogs that greet inappropriately might lunge, bark, or jump at other dogs or people because they haven't been taught a polite greeting. They might become frustrated because a leash is holding them back, taking away their autonomy and stopping their ability to act naturally. Similarly, a leash-reactive dog might be nervous on leash and react to keep stimuli he fears away from him.

The dog that barks and runs up and down the boundary of his fence might be doing so because he is bored or fearful of people on the other side. He might be warning them to stay away or telling you that someone is about to invade your territory. Dogs that are "contained" behind electric fences can see as well as hear stimuli beyond the boundary. This encourages them to bark and chase moving objects, such as cars or bicycles. They might be chasing these stimuli to get them away from their property or chasing them because it's a fun and reinforcing game.

These reactive types of behaviors shouldn't define your dog's personality. Labels place individual dogs into stereotyped groups and often cloud a person's perceptions and understanding of their own dogs. But regardless of what labels are used, intense, reactive types of behaviors can be dangerous for both dogs and people and should be addressed immediately by a certified dog trainer and behavior professional.

Reactive dogs are not bad dogs. They simply display problematic behaviors and emotional issues that need to be addressed using positive management and training techniques. Sometimes reactive behavior can turn into aggressive behavior, especially if your dog is insecure or doesn't understand or feel comfortable in a social situation. Aggression can also be elicited by a socially mature dog that doesn't welcome a lunging, barking, crazy adolescent coming toward them even if it's just to say hello.

Not all reactivity is fear based. Some dogs will learn to overreact on their own or by watching other dogs. It's normal for dogs in multidog households to pick up positive and negative behaviors from their housemates. It's also common for dogs to "self-learn."

Take the dog who barks at the mailman or delivery person as he delivers a parcel to your mailbox or front door. The dog spies the "intruder" and barks as the delivery man approaches the house. Once the mail or parcel has been delivered, the man moves away to the next house. As he moves away, the dog is still barking and continues to bark until the man is out of sight. The same thing happens each day at a similar time. The dog is consistently reinforced for barking because the man moves away from the home every time the dog barks. It doesn't matter to the dog if the man walks away for some reason other than a barking dog; walking away means that the dog has done his job. The dog might have initially felt some stress when the delivery person approached the house, but the daily reinforcement he gets from being successful is enough for him to wait by the window for the delivery person to come again. Positive reinforcement strengthens learning, even when it's something you don't want your dog to learn.

MANAGING THE REACTIVE ADOLESCENT

Reactive dogs should be seen by a veterinarian to make sure that they aren't reacting because of pain or other medical reasons. If there is no medical cause, your vet might recommend medication or other natural therapies to lessen your dog's stress. Once you determine that there is no underlying health condition, you can move on to management.

Some reactive dogs live very happy lives with management alone because they are never put in a position where they encounter the stimulus that triggers the behavior. This can be easy for people to implement as long as there is consistency. You can use baby gates, doors, noise, and visual barriers to separate your dog from the stimulus. You can give your dog problem-solving toys to distract her and give her something else to do or use harnesses or muzzles to keep her and others safe when she's outside.

In reactivity cases, other than physical tools such as muzzles and leashes, the easiest tool to use is space. Keeping a dog a certain distance from the problem stimuli can lessen or even eliminate the problem behavior. The key is to find your dog's critical distance, or the distance at which she perceives, processes, and responds to stimuli.

TRAINING THE REACTIVE ADOLESCENT

This is where I recommend again that you get a certified positive trainer in to help you, because defining the exact triggering stimulus and working on strategies to change behavior is vital and has to be done correctly and safely.

If your dog is a frustrated greeter, the trainer will work with you to teach your dog to greet appropriately, which might take some time depending on how intense his reaction is. If your dog is not fearful of others, success is very high as most dogs just need to learn the rules of a polite greeting. Reacting out of fear could be a potential bite risk to the triggering stimuli, so the emphasis needs to be on safety while a behavior modification plan is put into place.

There are three threshold points that are different for every dog:

1. Sensory threshold is the point at which the dog becomes aware of the stimulus.

2. Aversiveness threshold is the point at which the dog finds the stimulus aversive in some way.

3. Response threshold is the point at which the dog feels he has to respond to the stimulus.

Some dogs will find something aversive from a long distance away while others need to be closer to the stimulus to feel uncomfortable. Some dogs will respond immediately and others will take a while to do so. It is up to you to find your dog's sensory threshold and then work within your dog's comfort level.

Behavior modification techniques will help your dog feel differently about something that has previously made him uncomfortable. The beauty of positive training is that this can be done without the use of forceful and intimidating techniques, but it has to be done right and with a qualified professional.

Neutering

Neutering means that a dog's reproductive organs are removed resulting in sterilization. The sterilization of females is referred to as spaying, and males as neutering, but neutering also refers to both sexes.

When a female dog is spayed, her ovaries and uterus are removed via incisions made in her abdomen. Some dogs will just have an ovariectomy (removal of the ovaries only), which can be performed laparoscopically. In males, both testicles are removed from the scrotum through a small incision. In many countries, neutering dogs is uncommon unless the procedure is deemed medically necessary, but in the United States, neutering is a common practice primarily as a means for population control.

Most veterinarians recommend that the surgery be performed when the dog is between six and nine months of age, before the dog reaches sexual maturity. Others recommend that dogs should not be spayed and neutered until they are fully grown at about two years of age, but many shelters and rescues are neutering dogs younger than six months as a way to ensure that dogs leaving the rescue are never able to reproduce.

While virtually everyone agrees that neutering dogs is the best means of population control, experts still don't agree about the best age to neuter and how neutering impacts a dog's physical and mental health.

Early neutering can solve the inconvenience of a heat cycle and may prevent certain diseases, such as mammary cancer, but it can also deprive dogs of hormones that are necessary for normal skeletal growth and closure of the growth plates.

Neutering male dogs eliminates a small risk of testicular cancer and reduces the risk of noncancerous prostate disorders as well. It may reduce the risk of perianal fistulas and diabetes but significantly increases the risk of osteosarcoma (a common bone cancer in medium and large breeds) if done before a year old. It can triple the risk of hypothyroidism, geriatric cognitive impairment, and obesity as well as cause issues in bone growth if done too early.

Spaying female dogs greatly reduces the risk of mammary tumors if done before two and a half years of age. Mammary tumors are the most common malignant tumors in female dogs. It nearly eliminates the risk of pyometra (an infection of the uterus), which affects about 23 percent of intact female dogs, reduces the risk of perianal fistulas, and removes the very small risk of uterine, cervical, and ovarian tumors. Spaying can significantly increase the risk of osteosarcoma if it's done before a year old, as well as other cancers and heart problems. I have seen quite a few female dogs that have urinary "spay incontinence" as well as recurring urinary tract infections.

BEHAVIORAL EFFECTS

The behavioral effects of neutering have also been widely studied. Some positive behavioral effects include a reduction in roaming, urine marking, and mounting in male dogs. Contrary to conventional wisdom, studies seem to indicate that neutering might slightly increase aggressive, fearful, and reactive behavior as well as cause noise sensitivity in some dogs. Some experts believe these adverse effects on behavior may be due to the loss of hormones resulting in a conflicted emotional state.[2]

Scent Marking

Puppies have toileting accidents even when they are housetrained, and this can be incredibly frustrating for you. But however annoyed you might feel, don't blame your pup. Puppies aren't being stubborn or spiteful if they have an accident, they just might forget, feel unwell, or be responding to some kind of stress or change in their environment. It's up to you to find out the cause, alleviate any stress your puppy might have, and teach him what you want him to do.

There are many reasons why dogs toilet in the home, and one of the most common is no accident at all. Scent marking is different from a housetraining problem. Dogs that scent mark often leave urine in many different places around the home and outside in small quantities. Toileting accidents tend to produce larger amounts of urine in one area.

Once you have ruled out any medical cause for the behavior, it's time to tackle scent marking. It's not an easy thing to stop, but it helps to understand why dogs scent mark and how you can stop the need to do so.

Scent marking is when your dog leaves urine, feces, or other bodily fluids on an object, in the air, or on the ground. Any object, piece of furniture, bush, stone, animal, or person can be marked and dogs will do this in a variety of ways. Male dogs tend to lift a leg and mark vertical surfaces. Female dogs will sometimes lift a leg, but tend to squat and leave a dribble of urine on the ground.

Male and female dogs will also mark with feces, leaving poop on a raised clump of grass or on a stone—perfect placement close to nose height for other dogs to come along and sniff this olfactory flag. Call it small-dog syndrome, but some small dogs, like Chihuahuas, are known to do handstands while they spray urine or poop, leaving their calling card higher so it's easier for other dogs to read and maybe fooling neighborhood sniffers that a larger dog was in the area.

Dogs can be very inventive when it comes to marking objects, especially when it's a person. The person standing in a dog run watching their dog play or chatting idly to a friend might not notice a dog come by and lift a leg to spray their shoes. Someone sitting on the couch might mistake marking as the dog being affectionate when he swipes past them or rubs his face or body against their legs. Cats are not the only animals that spread scent by rubbing their faces against you.

Wolves are known to mark territory by urinating on boundary lines, but dogs tend to mark and countermark isolated areas where other dogs have been, raised areas, or objects, rather than marking their territory. There are some working dogs, however, that will mark their territorial boundaries with urine. Anatolian shepherd dogs in Namibia warn cheetahs and other wild animals to stay away from flocks of goats or sheep they protect by urinating on bushes, rocks, and other raised areas around the flock as they feed. These boundaries change as the flock moves and the dog moves with them. Predators tend to stay away from these dogs that use scent and their sheer size to intimidate.

Jasmine is a marker and follows Sadie around on a walk, urinating on anything that Sadie urinates on. Maybe they are both leaving information about each other for the neighborhood dogs to sniff later on.

OTHER TOILETING ISSUES

If your dog is toileting in the home and you rule out scent marking, then there might be a medical reason for the behavior. A checkup at the veterinarian's office will help rule out many different medical conditions that contribute to housetraining problems, including gastrointestinal disease, urine infections, renal failure, or canine cognitive dysfunction.

If your dog is given a clean bill of health, you need to ask yourself if anything significant has happened with your situation in the last few weeks or if your dog's environment has recently changed. Did you move or did someone move in or out of your household? Did you get another pet or lose one? Have there been any familial disagreements that might affect your puppy or dog's behavior? Dogs are discerning creatures and are often affected by changes in their environment including moving, changes in family life (human and animal), changes in routine (nutrition, exercise, enrichment), or the addition of aversive training methods and tools.

The next thing to look at is your dog's toileting habits. Does your dog eliminate only during thunderstorms or when you leave? Does she eliminate when you come in from a walk or the yard? Does your dog sneak away to do her business in the same place? Finding a pattern can help identify why your dog is toileting. For example, dogs are prompted to go where other dogs have eliminated and ammonia can trigger this response. Since many household cleaners use this chemical, look for an enzymatic, natural cleaner.

The best way to encourage appropriate toileting is to get back to the basics of potty training: active supervision, careful management, a consistent routine, and a little bit of training. Start with a good toileting schedule that allows access to outside areas every hour. Take your dog outside to eliminate after waking, eating, drinking excessively, playing, training, napping, and if you see the "potty dance" (sniffing, circling, hunching, or leg lifting). Encourage your dog to toilet with a verbal cue such as "go potty"; saying this cue while your dog eliminates will associate the word with the action. When your dog has finished toileting, praise her and remain outside for at least a few minutes. This way, your dog will not associate elimination with going inside and ending the fun!

If you catch your dog in the act of toileting inside, verbally interrupt her and take her outside to finish up. Try not to scare her with your interruption so that she still feels confident toileting in front of you when you are both outside. If you didn't catch your dog in the act of toileting, it's too late to redirect her and you should never rub her nose in an accident. Punishment causes stress that might encourage your dog to toilet even more. Punishment also teaches your dog that eliminating in front of you has bad consequences, so eliminating in secret is much safer. If your dog doesn't eliminate on leash but loves walking, take her out on the leash in the morning (even in the backyard) and praise her for going while the leash is attached.

Feed your dog at set times so you can predict when she might need to toilet, and limit water after a certain time in the evening if your dog is having accidents at night. Ice cubes can help your dog take water in at a slower pace while still quenching her thirst. Gradually decrease the frequency of trips outside as your dog builds up control. Follow a schedule that builds up a predictable and reliable routine and be patient and sensitive as your dog learns.

Rearrange or manage your dog's environment to set her up for success and keep your house pee- and poop-free! Actively supervising your dog is the key to successful potty training, but supervision means watching your dog all the time. If you are unable to actively supervise your dog, she will need to be crated or confined to a smaller space. Use leashes, baby gates, bathrooms, and crates to confine your dog when you can't supervise her; however, be sure that she is receiving sufficient exercise and mental stimulation when not confined to avoid destructive behaviors and loneliness. Brain games, puzzles, and play are a great place to start.

Humping

Humping is a much misunderstood behavior. Many owners think that humping is a purely sexual activity, but mounting and humping happens when dogs get excited, aroused, and anxious, which has nothing to do with sex. Humping generally occurs when a dog mounts another dog and moves his or her rear in a repetitive motion. This behavior is considered "normal" dog behavior during play but can be abnormal when performed to extremes in other circumstances.

Many dogs hump from excitement when a person or fellow housemate comes home. Other dogs may hump because the behavior has been conditioned and reinforced over time. Whatever the cause, most people are annoyed and embarrassed when their dogs hump. It might be cute when a puppy humps something, but this quickly becomes a serious problem as the puppy grows. If you don't want your puppy to hump, you must break the reinforcement cycle in that situation. Unfortunately, humping is often reinforcing by itself without human intervention, so you have to do what you can to prevent humping in any situation.

Start by identifying the situations in which humping occurs, and make a plan to prevent the behavior by using short-term management solutions.

MANAGEMENT SOLUTIONS

One of the best ways to solve a humping problem is to manage the environment so your dog doesn't have access to what she likes to hump. When a dog can't practice a behavior, the behavior is likely to go into extinction. Here are some ways to manage your dog's environment:

- Remove your dog entirely by placing a barrier between him and the person, animals, or object he likes to hump. The barrier could be a baby gate, crate, or door.

- Keep your dog away from the stimulus by keeping him on a tether or leash when the stimulus is present.

- Remove the stimulus entirely by asking a visitor to walk away from your dog.

- Provide another stimulus (toss treats or a toy).

- Always consider checking in with your veterinarian, as humping can be a compulsive disorder or way of relieving anxiety.

TRAINING SOLUTIONS

Many owners complain about their dogs humping, but they rarely know what they would like their dog to do instead. You can curb humping by doing the following:

- Once you have verified that the humping is not from a serious medical condition, focus on something else that your dog can do instead of humping.

* Managing humping is key to preventing reinforcement. If your dog is humping out of boredom, provide extra enrichment that will replace humping behavior by providing outlets in other ways.

* Teach replacement behaviors to humping. You can teach your dog to find a toy or search for food while in the same area of the person or object your dog likes to hump. This will divert your dog's energy onto something more appropriate.

Mine!

Start teaching your puppy to drop objects from her mouth when you ask, as soon as she comes into your home. If your puppy or adult dog picks an object up and runs away from you, try not to run after her or be confrontational and threatening because you will make the situation a lot worse. Chasing is a fun game for some pups, and if this game is reinforcing, they will find more opportunities to play it.

Turn confrontation into a game of trade by teaching the "take it" and "drop it" cues, and your dog will feel a lot better about giving up an object. Here's how you teach it:

* Start with a low-value toy and present it to your pup. When she opens her mouth to take the object, say "take it."

* Allow your puppy to play with the object for a little while and then present her with a similar toy that you have behind your back.

* As your puppy drops the object she has in her mouth, say "drop it" and reward her with the one you have in your hand, saying "take it."

❧ Keep repeating this exercise until your pup is responding well to your cues. When she has mastered the technique, you can gradually build up to toys and objects that are of higher value.

If you are in a crisis situation and your dog won't give up the chicken bone or remote control she has been chewing, try playing the "go find it" game described on page 143:

❧ Start by dropping small high-value treats on the ground where your puppy can see you and tell her to "go find" the treats.

❧ Drop the treats on the opposite side of you so that your puppy has to run past you to get to the food. Gently retrieve the object as she is eating.

❧ You can help your pup love the "go find it" game by teaching the game to her in normal circumstances so that she doesn't only associate it with taking something she shouldn't.

This exercise doesn't reward your pup for stealing something but lowers her perception of threat, focuses her mind on something that makes her feel good, and prevents both of you from getting into a situation that could be dangerous. The best way to prevent your puppy from guarding an object is to manage your environment so she doesn't get the chance to take things she shouldn't, and teach her that giving things up from her mouth is a positive, fun thing to do. If your pup takes some food and won't drop it, resist the temptation to shout at her. If the food is not going to harm her, walk away and let her eat it, but if it's a household object or something that could harm her if ingested, implement a distraction by ringing the doorbell or taking her leash out to signal a walk. This usually refocuses a pup's mind onto better things and encourages her to release the object as she now anticipates something more exciting.

Muzzle Training

Every dog, regardless of temperament, should be taught to wear a muzzle. Puppyhood is the best time to start habituating pups to having their faces and mouths handled, as well as getting them comfortable with the feeling of having something on their face that restricts the movement of their mouths. This is especially important not just for vet visits where even the most docile of dogs can have a bad reaction, but for any situation where a dog might feel fear or pain and react negatively.

While muzzles are vital safety tools, they can also cause untold amounts of stress for dogs that are not used to wearing them. The sudden restriction of facial movement and mouth confinement can cause panic in the calmest of dogs as their primary method of defense is taken away. Not only that—certain muzzles can restrict breathing—making it very hard for dogs to breathe normally and to cool themselves down.

Teaching any dog to wear a muzzle should be a slow, careful process, as it's especially important to do things right, particularly with dogs that are nervous or don't like being handled around the mouth or face.

To begin, make sure you choose the right muzzle for your dog. This sounds like common sense, but it's shocking how many muzzles I have seen that don't fit properly or close the mouth completely for long periods of time. A perfect muzzle is one that fits snugly and comfortably and doesn't restrict your dog's natural functions, such as panting. A groomer's mesh or cloth muzzle is useful while your dog is being groomed or at the vet, but it should only be used for short periods and only worn when your dog can be continually supervised. Muzzles that close the mouth completely can be very dangerous, especially when your dog is exercising or feels unwell. A basket muzzle is the best option for most dogs and allows your dog to open his mouth to pant, drink water, take a treat, or vomit without the danger of aspiration.

Don't make the common mistake of only putting the muzzle on when your dog is in a situation or environment that makes him uncomfortable—in the presence of strangers or when there are loud noises, for example. The key to successful acclimation is to pair the muzzle with good things and fun experiences, rather than making the muzzle the predictor of "bad" or "scary" experiences. Once that is done, the muzzle can be worn when needed.

To help your puppy or adult dog adapt to a muzzle, bring it out for him to investigate and pair his investigation with a favorite treat or toy. Do not attempt to put the muzzle on at this point. Simply present, treat, and remove the muzzle from view. You do not need to use very high-value treats or toys at this stage, but make sure these good things only happen when the muzzle is present.

When you notice your dog is relaxed or excited when the muzzle is presented, you are ready to move on to the next level. Fasten the muzzle around your dog's neck like you would a normal collar. Do not put your dog's snout in the muzzle at this stage but let that part of the muzzle hang below your dog's head. While the muzzle is fastened there, continue to provide favorite treats that stop as soon as the muzzle is removed. Start by fastening the muzzle for short periods of time, and gradually build the time the muzzle is worn as your dog becomes more comfortable.

Once your dog is comfortable, it is time to begin the process of habituating him to putting his nose inside the muzzle basket. To start, cup your hand around the basket and place high-value food inside it. Do not force your dog's nose inside the basket but allow him to work out how to get the desired food from inside the muzzle at his own pace. Use additional food that you can feed through the muzzle to keep your dog's nose voluntarily in the basket for longer and longer periods.

You can also place the muzzle on the ground with some peanut butter inside and allow your dog to put his own head in it to get to the peanut butter. This gives more sustained reinforcement than individual treats. Remember to pick the muzzle up and put it away when he is finished so he does not start chewing on the actual muzzle itself.

Once your dog is comfortable with keeping his nose voluntarily inside the muzzle to receive rewards, you can begin touching your dog's head like you would if you were to fasten the head strap, if there is one, while the dog's nose is in the muzzle. Do not actually fasten the strap, though—simulate the sensation that your dog would experience if you were to fasten it.

After you have successfully acclimated your dog to this step, you can fasten the strap loosely and keep the muzzle on for very short periods. If you are teaching with a basket muzzle, keep high-value food flowing during the time your dog is wearing it, or just give plenty of praise for grooming muzzles where treats cannot be delivered. Make sure to remove the muzzle before your dog becomes uncomfortable or panicked by the new sensation.

It is important that you don't move too quickly through these stages as any progress you make could be damaged by taking a stage too fast and forcing your dog to do something he doesn't want to do. If your dog tries to get the muzzle off, distract him with a favorite treat or fun game and take him for a walk as long as he is wearing a basket muzzle. Only remove the muzzle when your dog is not actively trying to remove it himself with his head or paw.

Keep the teaching fun! Your ultimate goal is for your dog to make a positive association with the muzzle. This teaching process should not occur during a single training period. Work in short, fun training sessions of about ten to fifteen minutes each, and if you feel your dog becoming agitated, frustrated, distracted, or uncomfortable at any time, take a break or go back to the previous step and build up the association again. Keep the training light and fun, and your dog should run to put his face in the muzzle anytime you bring it out for him to wear.

Providing Enrichment

The brain is the most underused "muscle" in pet dogs. While dogs need appropriate physical exercise, many people fail to enrich their dogs' lives with mental and cognitive stimulation. This becomes most evident when a pet dog is going through adolescence, and when most people are challenged with their dog's behavior.

Left to their own devices, dogs will scavenge, hunt, roam the neighborhood, mate with other dogs, mark things that are important to them, and protect things of value. These are not appropriate behaviors in the human world, but lack of appropriate enrichment can lead to the development of stereotypical behaviors, such as incessant barking, inappropriate chewing, hyperactivity, and intense licking.

Environmental enrichment should provide both positive mental and physical experiences for your dog but shouldn't be overly stressful.

Solving puzzles can be intrinsically rewarding. Dogs that voluntarily work on puzzle toys or other enriching activities are much more fulfilled because just seeking something is intrinsically rewarding.

Nose-driven games like scent work and the "go find!" and "go seek!" games (see page 143) engage the entire cycle of the reward system. The reward system is a group of neural structures that includes desire (the seeking system) and pleasure (the consummatory system). The seeking system is an essential part of the reward system and is an important part of the emotional and behavioral well-being of all dogs. Training, exercise, food puzzles, dog sports, and other activities provide physical and mental stimulation for dogs of all ages and are especially beneficial for dogs that have behavioral issues.

AFTERWORD: LIVING IN HARMONY WITH YOUR DOG

Everyone wants their dog to be a friendly, obedient, and well-behaved member of the family. By the time puppies reach adulthood, they should be fluent in certain behaviors, such as walking well on the leash, sitting on cue, lying down, and coming when called. Behaviors that require impulse control are harder for young dogs, and there is certainly a chance that dogs will develop other challenging behaviors as they grow.

It is a good idea to get a certified positive trainer in to help you if you haven't already. A good trainer will teach your dog more life skills and find out why a particular behavior is happening. They will give you an effective management and teaching plan to help modify unwanted behaviors and enhance positive behaviors. They will find quick solutions by looking at where you live and where you go. They will also help manage your expectations and work with you to find solutions so that you and your dog can live in harmony together.

Realistic Expectations

So what do you expect from your dog at this stage? Do you want her to greet people politely, toilet outside, listen to you every time you ask her to do something, walk well on the leash, and come back when called? Do you want your dog to be a companion for your family, protect your home, and be friendly to other people and dogs she encounters?

Maybe your dog can't meet all these expectations, but teaching her life skills is all about getting her close to them. Don't forget that while you're teaching your dog, she also comes with her own set of expectations. When we bring a dog into our home, we take on a big responsibility. Your dog's behavior is a combination of genetics, learning, and environment, and you must never forget that she is constantly learning even when you are not actively teaching her. When you understand how your puppy and adult dog perceive the world, it is easier to appreciate why she behaves in a certain way. Your dog doesn't know right from wrong unless you teach her, because she thinks more in terms of what is safe and unsafe. It is up to you to teach her what is and what is not acceptable in your world.

Teach an Alternative

If your young dog's behavior is still too much to handle, build a support system around you. Maybe your dog can benefit from a few days at doggy day care, or you can hire a dog walker to help with daily walks. If your dog lunges at other dogs on walks, work with a trainer to teach him good leash and greeting skills rather than skipping walks. If your dog runs riot in the dog park, don't take him to the park until he learns to play more appropriately in calmer environments.

Always have a goal behavior to work toward. Once your dog understands what you want him to do, he will begin to offer behaviors without your having to ask for them. These behaviors will become so deeply ingrained that they become part of his ritual. When I get my dogs' leashes out of the drawer, for example, my dogs automatically stand calmly waiting for me to attach their leashes because a walk doesn't start until they're calm. When we come to the side of a road, my dogs know they have to stand and wait by the curb until I tell them we are going to cross the road. I prefer they stand, which is much more comfortable for them than having to sit all the time. When someone comes to my door, Sadie goes to get her toy before greeting them instead of sticking her nose between their legs to say hello.

If you are going to teach certain cues like "sit," "down," "come," and "stay," make sure you know why you're teaching them and don't overuse them. Cues serve an important function:

- ❧ Sitting is good for self-control.

- ❧ Lying down is good for relaxing.

- ❧ Coming when called is an important safety cue.

- ❧ Polite leash walking means a life of enjoyable walks.

- ❧ "Wait" means don't run out the door when I open it.

- ❧ "Attention" means look at me when I call your name.

- ❧ "Leave it" keeps your dog safe when you are walking outside.

- ❧ "Go potty" teaches your dog to toilet when asked.

Knowing what comes next is vital for your dog's success and happiness. Finding that all-important bridge between you and your dog's expectations will allow you to live confidently together. A dog that knows what is expected is far more welcome in our human world than one that is out of control.

Being Stubborn

I've lost count of the number of times I've heard people call their dogs stubborn. If your dog doesn't respond to a cue, you have to explore why rather than labeling and anthropomorphizing her intent. Dogs don't "do" stubborn, but pet parents are often quick to blame them, when in reality their dogs don't know what is required or don't feel comfortable doing what is asked. I see this when prospective clients tell me their dogs stubbornly put on the brakes during a walk. When I observe the behavior, I find that something very different is going on. Some dogs don't feel well while others are insecure outside. Some dogs don't like walking outside when it's too hot or too cold.

If your dog doesn't respond to you, she might not have heard you or understood what you are asking her to do. Ask yourself if you have taught her properly and if she has learned to respond in all kinds of situations. Your dog might sit beautifully in the kitchen but doesn't generalize that action to other environments. It's important to teach her to respond in all kinds of situations and with distractions, because it's hard for her to listen when there is too much going on around her.

Be Your Dog's Advocate

A confident dog is a joy to behold. Confidence is the feeling of self-assurance arising from an appreciation of one's own abilities or qualities. You can determine your dog's level of confidence by observing his body language and how he responds to different situations. It's important to look at his head, body, and tail to get a full picture of his emotional state and to observe his body signals in context with the environment he is in at the time. Yawning might mean he is tired late at night, but it could mean he is stressed during the day when he is surrounded by screaming children.

Confident dogs have neutral ears, soft eyes, loose bodies, and neutral or slightly raised tails. You can build your dog's confidence by giving him choice, managing his environment, playing with him, helping him learn, and giving him the life skills he needs to be successful.

Be aware of your dog's body language and protect him from overwhelming situations. Your dog can't speak up for himself so you must advocate for him. Jasmine doesn't like children approaching her, so I make sure that I walk away from areas where children are likely to be, and I manage her space if a child does want to pet her. Sadie is a social butterfly with people but isn't that comfortable with other dogs, so I don't take her to dog parks or other places where I know she can get overwhelmed. If we find ourselves in a situation that is too overpowering, we turn around and make a quick exit. I have taught both my dogs an "emergency u-turn" that can be utilized if we find ourselves in an uncomfortable situation. I have taught the "turning" cue in a fun, positive way and use it in all kinds of fun situations so that it becomes a positive action that is reinforced when we're having fun. Because we have practiced this cue so much when the dogs are relaxed, it is highly effective when the dogs are stressed. The cue is predictable, and once I say it, my dogs know to turn around with me and walk off in the other direction, moving away from a potentially overwhelming situation.

Make Time

I'm a busy person. As well as filming my various shows, I run a business that takes up a lot of my time. I am also a mother and when I'm not on the road, my daughter's needs take precedence over everything else. I have a team that works with me, but my workload is still vast and it's hard to find the time to get everything done. I'm not complaining, but I think that sometimes my dogs do.

I have never been comfortable with having dogs just fit into my day. I fully admit that there are some times when I don't want to take them for a walk or play with them—there are so many other things I need to get done and it would be a lot easier if I had those extra hours each day to do them. However, I just don't feel right until my dogs have had daily exercise and all their needs have been attended to. I personally can't concentrate until I know they are fulfilled, which means I make sure a certain portion of the day is set aside just for them. I am responsible for making my dogs' lives the best they can be, and I encourage all my clients to try to do the same with theirs—making time for the animals in your life is essential for their physical and mental health.

Undesirable behaviors occur when dogs have little to no daily outlets. Many people bring dogs into their lives for selfish reasons and don't make the time to fulfill their dogs' needs. Consequently, these dogs spend long hours by themselves with nothing to do, forcing them to find their own ways of coping with boredom. All too often, the bored dog chews on household items, barks uncontrollably, or becomes reactive and anxious. Ultimately, the prescription for problem behaviors like these is an easy one—a simple modification protocol that includes more physical and mental enrichment. Advising my clients to utilize the tools I give them is the easy part, but the follow-through can be a lot harder.

If you've watched my show *It's Me or the Dog*, you will, on many occasions, have seen me shake my head in despair when after advising a family on the importance of enrichment and giving them a training plan, I return to a myriad of excuses as to why they didn't follow it. What amazes me is that they are mildly irritated that their dog is still behaving badly, as if it is somehow my fault. I'm sure there will be many trainers and other animal professionals reading this who have had similar experiences. And when I think I've heard every excuse, another one always comes along that is more far-fetched than the last.

One of my clients once told me that they didn't want to give their border collie too much exercise because that would only build up more strength and stamina and she would require more exercise. This dog was already climbing the walls in her urban household and without more outlets for her boundless energy and supercanine intelligence, the poor thing would go out of her mind and become even more of an irritant to her family.

Would You Pass?

If your dog could interview you before you brought her home to live with you, how would you convince her that you were the right home and family for her to spend the rest of her life with? Would you have passed the interview process? Could you offer her everything she needed? How do you think you measure up now to the promises you made when she was a puppy?

I love asking my clients these questions because it makes them think about what they have to offer and what they could improve. I know many dogs that could have avoided lives of interminable boredom if they had had the chance to interview a family before going to live with them. If my dogs sat me down and told me how they felt about me, I'm sure most of it would be good, but I would fail in certain areas even though they would give me a high score for trying. They would tell me that they love their walks, but not the way I stop Jasmine from rolling in fox or coyote poop. My dogs would probably ask if I could spend a little less time on my computer and more time curling up with them. Sadie would definitely demand more food, and both would appreciate a standing invitation to the dinner table. Jasmine would tell me how much she loves playing with the flirt pole, and both would thank me for loving them as much as I do and for giving them a safe and comfortable home.

They would also tell me that enrichment has made their lives fun, whether it is enjoying a walk, playing tug, socializing with other dogs and people, problem solving challenges I give them, chewing on their favorite chew toys, or eating the delicious food I provide for them. They love team activities as well as quiet together time. Finding the right balance has helped both of my dogs achieve a calm stability and has made our lives together a whole lot easier.

So throughout a busy workday my dogs get a morning and afternoon walk, or one long walk a day if I can't get to both. They have quiet time to recharge and then game time, which might involve vigorous play or problem-solving exercises like hide and go find. They have a daily activity/chew toy that is filled with part of their daily food allowance and the rest of their food is fed at mealtimes through a different and more complex puzzle/activity toy. In the evening they enjoy the simple yet much loved pleasure of just being close and cuddling up together.

I'm lucky, because there is always someone around in my household that can make sure my dogs get what they need if I'm not there, but even if your dog spends more time by himself, there are still ways to give him appropriate outlets throughout the day. Dog walkers, day care, durable chew toys, and calming music are just a few of the ways you can enrich his life when you are not there. If you work out of the house all day, you can try getting up a little earlier in the morning to exercise your dog and then hide toys and treats around the house so he can hunt for them while you are at work. (Care should be taken with the "hunt and go find it" game if you have a multidog household as disagreements can occur over resources such as food and toys.) A combination of these two activities can tire your dog out for hours and is a lot cheaper than hiring a dog walker or dropping a dog off at day care.

I am not the most organized person, but I work hard at being the kind of person I think my dogs want and need me to be. I seem to be on the right track, as my dogs are very happy. I know I don't always hit the mark for them, but where enrichment is concerned, I do my best to make sure they have as many outlets as they need. I waited a long time before I had dogs of my own, because I wanted to give them the best life possible. My dogs complete me and make my life better, and I work as hard as I can to do the same for them.

Our Beloved

It was inevitable, but we didn't want to face it. This book was written with Sadie and Jasmine by my side, but as I wrote it, I knew that my beloved Sadie was fading. She was a typical Labrador—a warrior of a dog that never showed her pain or discomfort, but I knew she was hurting and that we had done everything possible to help her. Old age had caught up and we could no longer ignore the fact that it was time.

Our beloved looked at us with her big eyes, and we knew we had to let her go. We had fought the arthritis that had plagued her for so long and tried to manage her pain, but we were losing the fight as Sadie came into her sixteenth year, and we knew her time was limited. In February, Sadie left this life, surrounded by the people who loved her and her best friend, Jasmine. She slipped away peacefully with our heads next to hers and with our hands touching her beautiful, chocolate brown fur.

Not long after Sadie had passed, Jasmine did what she always did and climbed onto Sadie's body to lie down. However, this time my bright-eyed, energetic Chihuahua was different. Jasmine was very slow and calm and as she lay down, her head rested quietly between her front legs. She stayed like that until it was time for Sadie to go. Jasmine knew her friend and anchor was gone.

Rest easy now, my beloved. You live on in our hearts and in the thousands of photos and videos we took of you. We smile at all the wonderful paintings, ornaments, plates, and crafts that people sent us over the years with your beautiful face painted on them, and most of all, we cherish the memories we have of the eleven years we were lucky enough to spend with you. May every puppy have your joyful energy, your kindness, and enjoy the love that you had, and may everyone who reads this book cherish each and every day they have with all the pups that come into their lives.

ACKNOWLEDGMENTS

This book has been a labor of love, and I couldn't have done it without my wonderful family. Thank you to my husband, Van Zeiler, and my daughter, Alex Zeiler, as well as friends and family that have supported me along the way. Thank you also to my incredible editor, Lisa Westmoreland, and everyone at Ten Speed Press—I couldn't ask for a better team to work with.

Thank you to Aly Lecznar for helping me research this book and to all the team at Positively, VSPDT, and VSA Academy—you inspire me. To all VSPDT graduates and students—I am so glad you decided to continue your journey with us, and I'm excited that so many people and dogs will benefit from your exceptional talents.

There are so many people who have motivated me, as well as dogs and puppies that have taught me so much. I feel blessed to have worked alongside amazing people in both the training and the rescue world. Thank you for everything you do to make the lives of dogs better. Kindness is indeed powerful!

RESOURCES

Official website ❧ www.positively.com

Find a trainer ❧ www.positively.com/trainers

Learn more about dog training and behavior ❧
www.vsdogtrainingacademy.com

Get a Positively No-Pull Harness ❧ www.positively.com/shop

Facebook ❧ www.facebook.com/victoriastilwell

Twitter ❧ @VictoriaS

Instagram ❧ @VictoriaStilwell

ENDNOTES

INTRODUCTION

1. V. LoBue et al., "Young Children's Interest in Live Animals," *British Journal of Developmental Psychology* (2013): 57–69.
2. S. Paulson et al., "The Thinking Ape: The Enigma of Human Consciousness," *Annals of the New York Academy of Sciences* 1303, no. 1 (2013): 4–24.
3. J. Topal, "Attachment Behaviour in Dogs: A New Application of the Ainsworth's Strange Situation Test," *Journal of Comparative Psychology* 112 (1998): 219–229.
4. E. Friedman et al., "Animal Companions and One-Year Survival of Patients After Discharge from a Coronary Care Unit," *Public Health Reports* 95, no. 4 (1980): 307–312.

CHAPTER 1

1. J. Serpell, "Early Experience and the Development of Behaviour," in *The Domestic Dog—Its Evolution, Behaviour and Interactions with People* (Cambridge, UK: Cambridge University Press, 1996): 79–102.
2. Ibid.
3. A. Gazzano et al., "Effects of Early Gentling and Early Environment on Emotional Development of Puppies," Department of Veterinary Anatomy, Biochemistry, and Physiology, University of Pisa, 2008.

4. E. Bray et al., "Effects of Maternal Investment, Temperament, and Cognition on Guide Dog Success," *Proceedings of the National Academy of Sciences of the USA*, 2017.

5. R. Coppinger and L. Coppinger, *Dogs: A Startling New Understanding of Canine Origin, Behavior, and Evolution* (New York: Scribner, 2001).

6. A. Gazzano et al., "Effects of Early Gentling and Early Environment on Emotional Development of Puppies," Department of Veterinary Anatomy, Biochemistry, and Physiology, University of Pisa, 2008.

7. J. Hekman, "How a Mother's Stress Can Influence Unborn Puppies," *Whole Dog Journal*, 2018.

8. F. McMillan et al., "Differences in Behavioral Characteristics Between Dogs Obtained as Puppies from Pet Stores and Those Obtained from Noncommercial Breeders," *Journal of American Veterinary Medicine* 242, no. 10 (2013): 1359–1363.

9. Humane Society of the United States, "99 Percent of Puppies Sold in Pet Stores Come from Puppy Mills and Backyard Breeders," 2016.

10. Interview with Abigail Witthauer, Roverchase, www .roverchase.com, 2018.

CHAPTER 2

1. S. Colman, "Can a Collar Damage a Dog's Thyroid?" *Whole Dog Journal*, 2019.

2. A. M. Pauli et al., "Effects of the Application of Neck Pressure by a Collar or Harness on Intraocular Pressure in Dogs," *Journal of American Animal Hospital Association* 42, no. 3 (2006): 207–211.

3. A. Hallgren, *Back Problems in Dogs: Underlying Causes for Behavioral Problems* (Stockholm, Sweden: AH Books, 2016).

4. R. Polsky, "Can Aggression in Dogs Be Elicited Through the Use of Electronic Pet Containment Systems?" *Journal of Applied Animal Welfare Science* 3, no. 4, (2000): 345–357.

5. N. Tudge, "The Use of Shock in Animal Training," Pet Professional Guild, 2016.

6. R. Coppinger and L. Coppinger, *Dogs: A Startling New Understanding of Canine Origin, Behavior, and Evolution* (New York: Scribner, 2001).

7. K. Uvnas-Moberg, "Role of Oxytocin in Human-Animal Interactions," People and Animals for Life, 12th International Association of Human-Animal Interaction Organization Conference (Stockholm, Sweden: 2010).

8. Y. F. Guzman et al., "Fear Enhancing Effects of Septal Oxytocin Receptors," *Nature Neuroscience* 16, no. 9 (2013): 1185–1187.

9. Australian Association for Infant Mental Health, "Controlled Crying," 2013.

10. Ibid.

11. Ibid.

12. E. McGee, "Separation Anxiety," Mississippi State University, College of Veterinary Medicine, 2016, www.cvm.msstate.edu/cvm-counseling-and-psychological-services/19-animal-health-center/367-separation-anxiety.

13. J. Dodds, "Dog Vaccine Protocol," Animal Health Foundation, 2017.

14. Ibid.

15. R. K. Anderson, "A Letter on Puppy Socialization," 2013.

16. L. Honeckman, Veterinary Behavior Solutions, www.veterinarybehaviorsolutions.net.

17. The Association of American Feed Control, www.aafco.org.

18. L. M. Freeman, "A Broken Heart: Risk of Heart Disease in Boutique or Grain-Free Diets and Exotic Ingredients," Clinical Nutrition Service, Cummings School of Veterinary Medicine, Tufts University, 2018, http://vetnutrition.tufts.edu/2018/06/a-broken-heart-risk-of-heart-disease-in-boutique-or-grain-free-diets-and-exotic-ingredients.

CHAPTER 3

1. J. Day et al., *Butler Biology Handbook*, 2000, http://
    kellyschwippert.weebly.com/uploads/3/7/3/2/37320053/
    biohandbook.pdf.
2. American Psychological Association, "Dogs' Intelligence on Par
    with Two-Year-Old Humans," *Science News*, 2009.
3. B. Turcsána, F. Range, et al., "Birds of a Feather, Flock
    Together? Perceived Personality Matching in Dog-Owner
    Dyads," *Journal of Applied Animal Behaviour Science*, 2012.
4. B. D'Aniello, "Dogs Obey Better to Gestural Than Vocal Stimuli
    by Strangers," University of Naples, 2016, www.researchgate
    .net/project/Human-dog-communication-2.
5. J. P. Scott, "The Evolution of Social Behavior in Dogs and
    Wolves," Department of Psychology, Bowling Green State
    University, Ohio, 1967.
6. S. Yin and B. McCowan, "Barking in Domestic Dogs: Context
    Specificity and Individual Identification," *Animal Behaviour*
    68, no. 2 (2004): 343–355, https://doi.org/10.1016/j.anbehav
    .2003.07.016.
7. T. Farago et al., "Inter and Intraspecific Vocal Communication
    of Dogs," Family Dog Project, Eötvös Loránd University,
    Budapest, Hungary, 2017.
8. P. Pongrácz et al., "Communicative Aspects of Dog Growls,"
    Family Dog Project, Eötvös Loránd University, Budapest,
    Hungary, 2017, http://familydogproject.elte.hu/staff.html.
9. Ibid.
10. J. Coulson, "The Negative Effects of Time-Out on Children,"
    Institute for Family Studies, 2016, https://ifstudies.org/blog/
    the-negative-effects-of-time-out-on-children.
11. M. Bekoff, "Social Play in Coyotes, Wolves, and Dogs,"
    Bioscience 24, no. 4 (1974): 225–230.

12. N. J. Rooney and J. W. S. Bradshaw, "Links Between Play and Dominance and Attachment Dimensions of Dog-Human Relationships," *Journal of Applied Animal Welfare Science* 6, no. 2 (2003): 67–94.

13. Ibid., 67–94.

CHAPTER 4

1. J. Hoomans, "35,000 Decisions: The Great Choices of Strategic Leaders," *Leading Edge Journal*, 2015, https://go.roberts.edu/ leadingedge/the-great-choices-of-strategic-leaders.

2. N. Jenner, "Positive Discipline: The Importance of Autonomy for Children," *Boundaries of the Soul*, 2012, https:// boundariesofthesoul.com/2012/10/15/positive-discipline-the-importance-of-autonomy-for-children.

3. W. Glasser, "Choice Theory," Glasser Institute for Choice Theory, 1970 wglasser.com.

4. D. Pink, "What Motivates Us?" *Harvard Business Review*, 2010.

5. M. Popova, "Autonomy, Mastery, and Purpose: The Science of What Motivates Us" (review of Daniel Pink, RSA animation), Brain Pickings, 2013, www.brainpickings.org/2013/05/09/ daniel-pink-drive-rsa-motivation.

6. Ibid.

7. B. Hare and V. Woods, *The Genius of Dogs—How Dogs Are Smarter Than You Think* (New York: Plume, 2013).

8. Ibid.

9. A. Huber et al., "Investigating Emotional Contagion in Dogs to Emotional Sounds of Humans and Conspecifics," *Animal Cognition* 20, no. 4 (2017): 703–715.

10. K. Guo et al., "Left Gaze Bias in Humans, Rhesus Monkeys, and Domestic Dogs," *Animal Cognition* 12, no. 3 (2009): 409–418.

11. Ibid., 409–418.

12. T. P. Alloway, "Working Memory Is a Better Predictor of Academic Success Than IQ," *Psychology Today*, 2010.

13. C. Fugazza et al., "Do as I Do . . . Did! Long-Term Memory of Imitative Actions in Dogs," Eötvös Loránd University, Budapest, Hungary, 2015.

14. A. Horowitz, *Being a Dog* (New York: Scribner, 2017).

15. Ibid.

16. J. Neitz, "Color Vision in the Dog," *Visual Neuroscience*, 2009, www.cambridge.org/core/journals/visual-neuroscience/article/color-vision-in-the-dog/5A30E35A384D10B6A2B46B01C896D3D5.

17. J. Leeds, "Through a Dog's Ear," www.throughadogsear.com.

CHAPTER 5

1. K. Overall, "Reactivity in Dogs," in *Clinical Behavioral Medicine for Small Animals* (Maryland Heights, Missouri: Mosby, 1997).

2. P. Farhoody et al., "Aggression Toward Familiar People, Strangers, and Conspecifics in Gonadectomized and Intact Dogs," Frontiers in Veterinary Science, 2018, https://www.frontiersin.org/articles/10.3389/fvets.2018.00018/full.

ABOUT THE AUTHOR

©KEVIN LOWERY

VICTORIA STILWELL is a world-renowned dog trainer and creator and host of the international hit television series *It's Me or the Dog*. She has served as a judge for CBS's *Greatest American Dog* and as the on-screen behavior expert for Oxford Scientific Films's *Dogs Might Fly*. Stilwell is also the creator, producer, and narrator of the Smithsonian Channel's *Dogs with Extraordinary Jobs*. Stilwell is the CEO of the Victoria Stilwell Academy for Dog Training and Behavior, editor in chief of the Positively website, founder of the global dog-trainer network VSPDT, and host of the *Positively* podcast series. She is the author of several bestselling books, including *It's Me or the Dog*, *Train Your Dog Positively*, and *The Secret Language of Dogs*. A leader in the field of animal behavior, Stilwell is a regular guest on talk shows, news broadcasts, and radio programs around the world and has been the recipient of multiple international awards and honors. She lives in Atlanta with her husband, daughter, and rescue dog, Jasmine.

INDEX

A

adenovirus, 51
adolescent dogs
  exuberant, 163–64
  fearful, 164–67
  impulsive, 167–74
  neutering, 178–80
  providing enrichment for, 191
  reactive, 174–78
aggression, 79
allergies, 56, 60
anal sac issues, 57, 141
anchoring, 161
appeasement signals, 91–92
"attention" cue, 194
auditory memory, 135–36
autonomy, 125, 128–29
aversiveness threshold, 178

B

"back up" cue, 169
barking, 45–47, 93–96, 175–76
begging, 168–71
behavior
  aggressive, 79
  boredom and, 191, 197
  definition of, 76
  dominance and, 74, 77–80
  early development and, 15
  exuberant, 163–64
  genetics and, 8–9, 16
  littermates and, 9–10

  management and, 67–68, 83, 86
  neutering and, 180
  personality and, 18–19
  puppy mills and, 21
  reinforcing desired, 27, 85
  stopping unwanted, 84–86
  teaching alternative, 82–85, 193–94
  understanding, 76–77
  See also individual behaviors
body language, 161, 195–96
bonding, 42–43
bones, 64
Bordetella, 49, 52
boredom, 191, 197
brain development, 13, 14–15, 46
breeders, licensed, 23–24
breeds
  behavior and, 8–9, 16
  choosing, 16–19
  communication and, 91
  types of, 16–18
  variations within, 16

C

canine influenza, 51
Canine Noise Phobia (CNP) series, 151
cats, 30–31
chewing, 98–101
chews, 64
choice
  autonomy and, 125
  -centered training, 156–60

power of, 44, 122–25, 129–30
stress and, 130–31
theory, 126
choke collars, 33–36
cognitive dimensions, five, 133–39
collars
choke, 33–36
nylon, 32
prong, 33–36
shock, 36–39
coming when called. *See* recall skills
communication
body language, 161, 195–96
canine intelligence and, 133–35
common mistake in, 86–87
consistency of, 68–69
human personality and, 87–88
by puppies, 91–92, 161
tone of voice and, 87, 88
See also barking; cues; growling
confidence, 68, 155–56, 195
corn, 58, 60–61
coronavirus, 52
corrections, 34, 35, 84–85
cortisol, 82, 166
cues
"attention," 194
"back up," 169
"drop it," 100, 104, 186–87
function of, 194
"go potty," 107, 194
"leave it," 194
nonresponse to, 90–91
"pick up," 69
problem solving and, 90–91
"quiet," 95
"speak," 95
"take it," 100, 186–87
teaching, 194
touch, 111–12
"turning," 196

vocal vs. physical, 88–90
"wait," 63–64, 164, 194
cunning, 138–39

D

DAPP vaccine, 49
DCM (dilated cardiomyopathy), 59–60
development
brain, 13, 14–15, 46
early, 8–14, 15
distemper, 51
dog food, 58–61
dog parks, 117–19
dogs
attraction of humans to, 5–6
being advocate for, 195–96
body language of, 195–96
bond between humans and, 42–43
emotions of, 6, 45, 133
expectations and, 192–93
expenses of responsible
ownership of, 15
health benefits of ownership of, 7
intelligence of, 132–39
introducing puppy to, 28–30
living in harmony with, 192–200
making time for, 196–97
providing enrichment for, 191
social play with other, 112–13
"stubborn," 194–95
wants and needs of, 198–99
wolf ancestry of, 42
See also adolescent dogs; behavior;
breeds; puppies; training
DogTV, 147–48
dominance, 74, 77–80
"drop it" cue, 100, 104, 186–87

E

ear infections, 56
e-collars, 36–39
electric fences, 38

emotions, 6–7, 45, 80–82, 133

empathy, 133

enrichment, providing, 191

episodic memory, 136–37

equipment, 32–39

estrus, 14

exercise, 7, 27, 41, 47, 100–101, 119–20, 197

F

family members, introducing puppy to, 26

fear

    in adolescent dogs, 164–67

    function of, 82

    period, 13–14

    preventing, 153–56

    recovery from, 67

    signals, 92

feeding, 58–64

fences, 38

fleas, 54

flu, 51

food allergies, 60

free feeding, 61

friends, introducing puppy to, 26

G

"go find" game, 143

"go potty" cue, 107, 194

"go seek" game, 144

greeting, 72–73, 171–74, 178

growling, 45–47, 71, 96–98

gundogs, 18

H

habituation, 69–70

handling issues, 70–72

harnesses, 32–33

health

    anal sac issues, 57, 141

    food and, 59

hot spots, 57

infections, 56–57

parasites, 54–56

puppy pyoderma, 57

vaccinations, 48–54

vet visits, 48, 70

hearing, sense of, 135–36, 149–51

heartworms, 55–56

herders, 17

hookworms, 56

hot spots, 57

housetraining, 104–8, 180–84

humping, 184–86

I

impulse control, 63–64, 167–74

infections, 56–57

intelligence, canine, 132–39

J

Jacobson's organ, 141

jealousy, 6

jumping, 171–74

juvenile period, 14

K

kennel cough. *See* Bordetella

kibble, 58–61

L

lap dogs, 18

leash skills, 120–21

"leave it" cue, 194

leptospirosis, 49, 52

lice, 55

life skills

    chewing, 98–101

    leash, 120–21

    nipping and mouthing, 101–4

    play, 112–14

    recall, 108–12

    social, 115–19

teaching, 65–66, 73–74

toileting, 104–8

walking, 119–20

livestock guardians, 17

M

management, role of, 67–68, 83, 86

memory, 135–37

mites, 55

mouthing, 98, 101–4

muzzles, 188–90

N

nail trimming, 71, 153

naps, 27

neonatal period, 10

neutering, 178–80

nipping, 101–4

noise phobias, 149–51

nose touch, 111–12

O

odor layering, 140

olfactory memory, 135–36

oxytocin, 43

P

parasites, 54–56

parvovirus, 51

personality, 18–19

pets, introducing puppy to, 28–31

pet stores, 21–22

"pick up" cue, 69

play skills, 112–14

positive training, 74–75, 79

predictability, role of, 68–69

primary socialization, 11–12

problem solving

cues and, 90–91

for puppies, 131, 137–38

rewards and, 126–27

prong collars, 33–36

puppies

adaptable, 66, 69–70

attraction of humans to, 5–6

autonomy for, 128–29

bonding with, 42–43

bringing home, 16, 25, 26–31

emotions of, 80–82

exercise for, 27, 47, 100–101

expectations and, 40–41

feeding, 58–64

handling, 70–72

personality of, 18–19

picking, 15–24

power of choice for, 44, 122–25, 129–30

problem solving for, 131, 138

resilience of, 15, 66–70

safety and, 25–26, 52–53

sensory experience of, 139–53

sleep and, 27, 45–47

wants and needs of, 39–40, 160–62

See also adolescent dogs; behavior; communication; development; dogs; health; socialization; training

puppy classes and play groups, 53, 116

puppy mills, 13–14, 19–22

puppy proofing, 25–26

puppy pyoderma, 57

Q

"quiet" cue, 95

R

rabies, 50

raw hides, 64

reactivity, 174–78

reasoning, 137–38

recall skills, 108–12

rescue dogs, 22–23

resilience, 15, 66–70

response threshold, 178

rewards
    power of, 85–86
    problem-solving and, 126–27
rolling, in smelly stuff, 145–46
roundworms, 56

S

safety, 25–26, 52–53
scent hounds, 17–18
scent marking, 180–82
scent training, 143–45
secondary socialization, 12–13
sensory threshold, 178
separation anxiety, 96, 162
sexual maturity, 14
shelters, 22–23
shock collars, 36–39
sight hounds, 17
sleep, 27, 45–47
smell, sense of, 135–36, 139–46
socialization
    definition of, 13
    importance of, 115
    primary, 11–12
    secondary, 12–13
    skills, learning, 115–19
    vaccines and, 53–54
social memory, 137
sound therapy, 150–51
spaying, 178–80
"speak" cue, 95
stress
    choice and, 130–31
    physical effects of, 82
    positive, 82
    signals, 92, 153
"stubbornness," 194–95

T

tail wagging, 13
"take it" cue, 100, 186–87
tapeworms, 56

taste, sense of, 148–49
terriers, 18
thyroid gland, 34
ticks, 55
toileting skills, 104–8, 180–84
touch
    cue, 111–12
    sense of, 152–53
toy breeds, 18
training
    balanced, 74
    choice-centered, 44, 122–25,
        129–30, 156–60
    dance analogy for, 83
    importance of, 75–76
    learning foundation for, 82–83
    over-, 44
    positive, 74–75, 79
    rewards and, 85–86
    traditional, 74
    See also behavior; cues; life skills
transitional period, 11
treats, 64
tug, 103–4, 114
"turning" cue, 196
TV, 147–48

U

urinary tract infections, 57

V

vaccinations, 48–54
vet visits, 48, 70
vision, sense of, 146–48

W

"wait" cue, 63–64, 164, 194
walking skills, 119–20
whining, 45–47
whipworms, 56
working group dogs, 18
working memory, 136